The Pedagogy of Real Talk

Second Edition

The Pedagogy of Real Talk

Engaging, Teaching, and Connecting With Students At-Promise

Second Edition

Paul Hernandez
Foreword by Tia Brown McNair

FOR INFORMATION:

Corwin

A SAGE Company

2455 Teller Road

Thousand Oaks, California 91320

(800) 233-9936

www.corwin.com

SAGE Publications Ltd.

1 Oliver's Yard

55 City Road

London EC1Y 1SP

United Kingdom

SAGE Publications India Pvt. Ltd.

B 1/I 1 Mohan Cooperative Industrial Area

Mathura Road, New Delhi 110 044

India

SAGE Publications Asia-Pacific Pte. Ltd.

18 Cross Street #10-10/11/12

China Square Central

Singapore 048423

President: Mike Soules

Associate Vice President
    and Editorial Director: Monica Eckman

Acquisitions Editor: Jessica Allan

Senior Content
    Development Editor: Lucas Schleicher

Associate Content
    Development Editor: Mia Rodriguez

Production Editor: Megha Negi

Copy Editor: Amy Hanquist Harris

Typesetter: C&M Digitals (P) Ltd.

Proofreader: Eleni-Maria Georgiou

Indexer: Integra

Cover Designer: Janet Kiesel

Marketing Manager: Olivia Bartlett

Copyright © 2022 by Corwin Press, Inc.

All rights reserved. Except as permitted by U.S. copyright law, no part of this work may be reproduced or distributed in any form or by any means, or stored in a database or retrieval system, without permission in writing from the publisher.

When forms and sample documents appearing in this work are intended for reproduction, they will be marked as such. Reproduction of their use is authorized for educational use by educators, local school sites, and/or noncommercial or nonprofit entities that have purchased the book.

All third-party trademarks referenced or depicted herein are included solely for the purpose of illustration and are the property of their respective owners. Reference to these trademarks in no way indicates any relationship with, or endorsement by, the trademark owner.

Printed in the United States of America.

Library of Congress Cataloging-in-Publication Data

Names: Hernandez, Paul (Sociologist), author.

Title: The pedagogy of real talk : engaging, teaching, and connecting with students at-promise / Paul Hernandez.

Description: Second edition. | Thousand Oaks, California : Corwin, 2022. | Includes bibliographical references and index.

Identifiers: LCCN 2021015686 | ISBN 9781071844816 (paperback) | ISBN 9781071844809 (epub) | ISBN 9781071844793 (epub) | ISBN 9781071844786 (pdf)

Subjects: LCSH: Children with social disabilities—Education—United States. | Education—Social aspects. | Educational psychology. | Communication in education. | Teacher-student relationships.

Classification: LCC LC4091 .H47 2022 | DDC 371.826/94—dc23

LC record available at https://lccn.loc.gov/2021015686

This book is printed on acid-free paper.

21 22 23 24 25 10 9 8 7 6 5 4 3 2 1

DISCLAIMER: This book may direct you to access third-party content via web links, QR codes, or other scannable technologies, which are provided for your reference by the author(s). Corwin makes no guarantee that such third-party content will be available for your use and encourages you to review the terms and conditions of such third-party content. Corwin takes no responsibility and assumes no liability for your use of any third-party content, nor does Corwin approve, sponsor, endorse, verify, or certify such third-party content.

Contents

Foreword Tia Brown McNair	vii
Preface	ix
Acknowledgments	xiii
About the Author	xiv

PART I: FOUNDATIONS	**1**
Chapter 1: Introduction	2
Chapter 2: PRT	11
Chapter 3: What Must Be True About You	29
Chapter 4: The Opportunity Gap, Demographic Shift, PRT, and a Sense of Belonging	57
PART II: IMPLEMENTATION	**71**
Chapter 5: Implementing Real Talk in the HEP Program	72
Chapter 6: Flexibility, Adaptability, and Effort	88
Chapter 7: Terministic Screens, Alternative Lessons, and Real Talk Discussions	96
Chapter 8: Implementing Real Talk in Any Classroom	109

PART III: TAKING PRT TO SCALE — 113

Chapter 9: Professional Development — 114

Chapter 10: Professional Development: Alternative Lessons — 132

Chapter 11: New Beginnings — 145

APPENDICES — 152

Appendix A:	Real Talk on Partnerships and an Alternative Lesson on Critical Thinking and Clinical Judgment	153
Appendix B:	Real Talk on Adversity and an Alternative Lesson on Chemical Bonding	156
Appendix C:	Real Talk on Doubt	159
Appendix D:	Real Talk on You Belong	162
Appendix E:	Real Talk on Symbolism	164
Appendix F:	"Who I Am" Real Talk on the First Day of Class	167
Appendix G:	Real Talk on Adversity	170
Appendix H:	Real Talk on Individuality in Learning	174
Appendix I:	Real Talk on Being Authentic	176
Appendix J:	Real Talk on Classroom Norms	178
Appendix K:	Examples of Real Talk Themes	180
Appendix L:	Bridge Project Packet	181
Appendix M:	Alternative Lesson on Congruent Triangles	192
Appendix N:	Alternative Lesson on Graphing Different Types of Linear Systems	199
Appendix O:	Alternative Lesson on Public Speaking Anxiety	206

References — 209

Index — 213

Foreword

Education is the most powerful weapon which you can use to change the world.

—Nelson Mandela

I had the pleasure of meeting Dr. Paul Hernandez when I was directing the Association of American Colleges and Universities' project *Committing to Equity and Inclusive Excellence: Campus-Based Strategies for Student Success*. He was serving as the Chief Diversity Officer at one of the participating campuses. As part of the project to examine and close equity gaps in student outcomes and educational designs, the team at the institution incorporated the Pedagogy of Real Talk (PRT) strategies. Paul's work inspired everyone in the room and left us wanting to learn more.

I reached out to Paul immediately and I have been inspired by his work ever since. I invited him to give a workshop at one of AAC&U's Diversity, Equity, and Student Success conferences. I believe it is important to share promising practices that can have impact on the success of students, especially historically marginalized and racially minoritized students. After his session at that conference, we had the opportunity to have lunch and to talk, and we did . . . for hours. Paul shared his story and what motivates him to engage in efforts to transform education into an environment where students, regardless of their backgrounds, can thrive and learn. I knew then what I still know today—he is more than a caring educator. He is *the* Real Talk educator.

The Pedagogy of Real Talk provides both a theoretical framework and practical guidance on a teaching strategy that centers the relationship between educators and students as a determining factor for student success. Paul's use of asset-based language to describe students and his understanding of how our lived experiences influence the ways in which we engage with our learning environments represent aspects of his story and the stories of so many students. PRT illustrates the importance of vulnerability, empathy, creativity, and grit as essential elements in creating an expansive learning environment for our students. We, as educators, have a responsibility to embrace our profession with a growth mindset in the same way we encourage our students to do so. Paul provides a roadmap for how that growth can happen.

This book was written for me, for you, and for any educator who understands the growing inequities in education and says, "No more." We have to expand our wheelhouse of proven strategies that can lead to sustained transformation and more students achieving their educational goals. We have to do more than just say we want change. Paul provides us with a guide on how to lead to achieve that change.

Tia Brown McNair, Ed.D.
Association of American Colleges and Universities
Vice President for Diversity, Equity, and Student Success and
Executive Director for the TRHT Campus Centers

Preface

It seems that just yesterday I was a little boy, growing up among gangs and in deep poverty with my single, immigrant momma. The discrimination we faced and that those like us continue to face creates seemingly insurmountable obstacles. I can remember, as a little boy, clenching my fists and closing my eyes, determined to survive because I simply wanted an opportunity.

Through most of my young life, I didn't view school as that opportunity. Instead, I viewed it as an obstacle. Had it not been for a few teachers, administrators, and staff who connected with me, my experiences and memories of school would have been only negative.

The voices and kindness of these people stayed with me as I left school, struggled through life, and eventually made my way to community college. College was hard because everything I didn't learn in school and what I did learn in the streets worked against me. I simply didn't think people like me belonged in school. The work was foreign and overwhelming, I felt like an impostor, and I expected to flunk out. Fortunately, a few professors, administrators, and staff took the time to understand how I learned. These dedicated individuals made all the difference in the world for me.

With their help, I found my rhythm and made my way through community college, earning an associate degree and transferring to a university. Nevertheless, the feeling of not belonging stayed with me throughout undergraduate and graduate school. Although I had many negative experiences in school, the positive ones had something in common. From elementary school through my doctorate, the educators who helped me develop a sense of belonging used similar approaches to engage with and teach me.

First, these caring educators were willing to be vulnerable and share their experiences with me, including how they felt through their own successes and struggles. This allowed me to see them as people and earned my trust. As I opened up to them, they were not judgmental or scared of me; instead, they were empathetic. I could tell that they cared sincerely about my personal well-being, and in return, I cared about them too.

Second, rather than seeing me as someone destined to fail, they had and fostered a growth mindset. They believed that they could develop ways to teach me effectively, and they thought I could succeed. I was a work in progress to them, and they wanted to contribute to my growth, which helped me build confidence in my abilities and develop my own growth mindset.

Additionally, these educators embedded creativity within how they taught and engaged me. As a result, I became a curious, interested participant and learned in a manner I never thought possible. My creativity was unleashed, both in school and out of school, helping me see beyond the life I was living.

Finally, they had grit. Although I said I wanted an opportunity to change my life, my actions sometimes said otherwise as I sabotaged my progress and pushed them away. I made things hard for them, yet they didn't walk away from me as many others had done throughout my life. Instead, to my surprise, they showed up every day and worked through the roadblocks. They could have gotten rid of me, but instead, they embraced me and displayed their grit. Through these amazing people, I successfully navigated and completed my formal education, and they are part of the inspiration for this book.

Since writing the first edition of *The Pedagogy of Real Talk*, I have continued to learn and to develop my pedagogy through my experience of the educators and students I have had the privilege to serve. This activity has included delivering professional development programs for many K–12 schools, universities, community colleges, and nonprofit organizations. I now refer to these programs as the Pedagogy of Real Talk (PRT) Institute. PRT provides an intensive, robust, and transformative experience that enables teachers[1] to learn, create, and implement my approach in their classrooms to increase student retention, persistence, grades, and completion rates and develop a sense of belonging.

In addition to teaching in the classroom, I have served as a chief diversity officer and, currently, as vice president of academic and student affairs, both within higher education. These positions have allowed me to further understand the broader context within which I seek to successfully apply institutional professional development that is teacher-led, sustainable, scalable, and supported by the administration. My work has earned awards and has resulted in opportunities I could have never imagined as a boy surviving on the streets. I was humbled to receive the Michigan Sociological Association Award for Outstanding Teaching for my work in classrooms. I was shocked and elated when I was invited to share my work through a TEDx talk. Recently, I was selected as a fellow of the Aspen Rising Presidents Fellowship within the Aspen Institute College Excellence Program. I have now reached a point where I feel compelled to write this second edition, reflective of my work's growth.

After my first book, I naïvely said I would not write another book. But five years later, I feel an even stronger obligation to write than before. In this edition, I have made updates throughout the book, removed sections and chapters from the first edition, and added chapters that I believe help to better capture the power of PRT. For example, Chapter 3 explains the need for vulnerability, empathy, growth mindset, creativity, and grit, as well as how teachers can embrace these concepts so as to implement PRT successfully in their classrooms. Chapter 4 discusses the opportunity gap, the demographic shift, and how PRT is fundamentally built to address all students' success and create a sense of belonging. Because my pedagogy was founded on work with our most vulnerable students, my book helps to reduce the opportunity gap within education.

I have also divided the book into three parts—Foundations, Implementation, and Taking PRT to Scale—to make using the book more efficient for you. As I mentioned in the first edition, PRT can be used in its entirety, in parts, or in conjunction with other approaches, and the new division into sections will help in this process. In Part 3, I have updated the training to reflect the robust professional development I conduct through the PRT Institute for all levels of education. Lastly, I have updated the conclusion and the appendices, describing the work of educators I have known over the last several years, so as to highlight the diversity, uniqueness, and personal nature of the various applications of PRT.

Every day, I see myself in the students who struggle to succeed in school. Although I "made it," my family continues to struggle within the environment from which I came. "Making it" also carries hidden burdens and demons that I did not expect and was not prepared for.

We have an obligation to ensure that our students succeed in school and to prepare them for successful careers and the continued challenges of life. PRT does not take away from the curriculum, nor is it "extra" work; instead, it is embedded in our teaching. The art and science of teaching begin with you. Develop your approach to teaching and then apply it to every student you encounter, especially our most vulnerable ones. We teach so that students can succeed, achieve their dreams, be happy, and live fulfilled lives.

Since my first book, many things have changed, including one particularly heartbreaking change that gave me a new perspective on and appreciation for life. My beloved mentor K. William Wasson passed away in 2018. He is one of the biggest reasons why I am alive today and enjoy the fortunate life I have. I remember one of our most special moments as we discussed my successful completion of the comprehensive exams in my PhD program. I could hear over the phone that his voice was different from usual. He said to me, "My friend, I prayed that I would get to see this day, and it has arrived. The student has become the teacher. Paul, you teach me more than I have ever taught you. You are now the teacher, my friend, and I look forward to continuing learning from you." To my surprise, I choked up, flooded with emotions, and told him that was impossible. I could sense him smiling as he continued, "Embrace your role and let go of the pain. Continue to grow and give away everything you learn so it can benefit others, especially those with the greatest needs."

I am eternally grateful for what my mentor gave me. I hope that this second edition ignites your passion as he ignited mine. Remember, the two most essential things in any school are (1) teaching and learning and (2) the supportive services we offer our students. And remember that equity and inclusion must be intentionally embedded within these actions.

Note

1. Although I generally refer to teachers, PRT can be used by instructors, professors, or any other professionals who work with students.

Acknowledgments

There are too many people to thank for supporting, believing, and encouraging me to write this second edition. I have not worked alone. Instead, it has been through collaboration with selfless, courageous, inspiring, and justice-driven colleagues committed to student success. Thank you all for being a positive force in my life. Additionally, Momma, my achievements are your achievements, and the good I have done in my life is a product of you. Lastly, to my mentor Bill, you saw in me what I could not see in myself: potential. There is no Dr. Paul Hernandez without you. Even after you passed in 2018, you continue to guide me with your words of wisdom—thank you, my friend.

About the Author

Paul Hernandez, PhD, earned his doctorate in sociology, specializing in the sociology of education, social inequality, and diversity. Dr. Hernandez is a nationally recognized speaker and leader in college access and success, community outreach, and pedagogy for educators working with underserved/underprepared students and students at-promise. As a former faculty member, nonprofit administrator, higher-education administrator, and educational consultant, Dr. Hernandez works with higher-education institutions, K–12 schools, and nonprofit organizations, helping them further develop and evolve their work with students and communities. Prior to earning his degrees, he was engulfed in gang culture and deep poverty, surviving on the streets of Los Angeles. Paul openly shares with others his unique personal story and how his path has influenced his work. He has learned ways to empower young people traveling a similar path, and through his inspirational messages, he hopes to share his lessons and passion with those working to address the multitude of challenges faced by diverse populations of youth at-promise. Dr. Hernandez has been nationally recognized for his work and was awarded the National

Education Association Reg Weaver Human and Civil Rights Award, the Michigan Education Association Elizabeth Siddall Human Rights Award, the Equity in Education Award by the Michigan Association of Collegiate Registrars and Admissions Officers, and an Honors Professor of the Year Award for teaching.

PART I

Foundations

Chapter 1: Introduction — 2

Chapter 2: PRT — 11

Chapter 3: What Must Be True About You — 29

Chapter 4: The Opportunity Gap, Demographic Shift, PRT, and a Sense of Belonging — 57

1 Introduction

When I was struggling in high school, administrators and teachers often spoke of me as a thing rather than as a person. They struggled to connect with me and my homeboys or to help us see a world beyond the Los Angeles ghettos. Rather than trying alternative methods to connect with students like us, teachers and administrators simply punished us and considered us a burden in the classroom. Eventually, I simply stopped going to school because education became my enemy rather than a source of empowerment to better my life. The feminization of deep poverty,[1] hunger, gangs, violence, and the social stigma of being different all contributed to my downward spiral within the education system. The manner in which I viewed the world and understood society, along with what I experienced on a day-to-day basis, was simply disregarded in the classroom. I was another student at-promise destined to drop out of school.

These experiences instilled a passion within me to create an alternative pedagogy to empower teachers to become more successful in working with students at-promise and, in turn, to increase passing rates for these students. I went from detesting school as a student at-promise to attaining my PhD. Today, my experience serves as a testament to the potential of students at-promise and as a reminder for teachers not to give up on their most challenging students.

Although academic success is crucial to being successful in American society, getting a job, owning a home, and reaching the middle class, students at-promise find succeeding in school difficult, if not impossible.

The negative experiences these students have in school and in their communities contribute to their poor performance, and their lack of academic success limits their opportunities for employment and educational growth. On a larger scale, their lack of success weakens the country overall. The nation needs more college-educated people to fill or to create much-needed jobs. Helping this population succeed is a major obstacle for teachers, a seemingly elusive goal—a goal that must be met!

However, in all the discussions centered on students at-promise, relevant solutions are rarely offered to teachers. Instead, the focus is on the conditions that lead to failure: the students' environment and the disadvantages they experience that result in their failure in school. Although it is important to identify these foundational issues to help students succeed, simply identifying them without creating applicable solutions for educators to incorporate in their classrooms is an injustice to teachers and students everywhere. Some even believe students at-promise do not want to learn, as reflected in one teacher's questions: "How do I teach students who do not seem to want to learn? How do I show them the importance of school when it seems like school just doesn't fit in with their lives?" Meanwhile, students at-promise mistakenly believe that school is not for them and that educators do not care about them.

My answer to this dilemma is PRT. Teachers can come to class with great ideas, interesting statistics, fascinating movies, and the coolest stories, but if there is no connection with this population of students, these approaches will fall on deaf ears because the students will not be receptive. Through PRT, teachers and students connect with curriculum through real-life experiences, allowing teachers to establish meaningful connections with students. As a result, students at-promise become receptive to learning from their teachers. PRT allows teachers to gain valuable insights into their students, something not usually possible with traditional approaches. As students become responsive to learning and as teachers gain insight into their students, the pedagogy then helps teachers create alternative lessons and assignments that connect students with the curriculum. The barriers between teachers and students at-promise crumble as new and exciting environments conducive to learning emerge to increase passing rates for students at-promise.

Students At-Promise

For several years, I have debated using the term "at risk" to describe students who struggle in school and appear headed toward dropping out. Though I used the term in an article I published in 2011, it didn't feel right then, and when I published my first edition of this book,

I began using "students at risk" as an alternative. I meant for this subtle change to convey that environmental risk factors impact students rather than insinuate students are the source of their vulnerable status. Still, the term "students at risk" is not a suitable replacement. Personally and professionally, I continue to struggle with how best to capture the complex needs, challenges, and, most importantly, our most vulnerable students' strengths. Thus, I have shifted to using the term "students at-promise" to reflect that, like all students, this population of students is full of potential for success (Dix et al., 2020; Osher & Kendziora, 2010; Sachar et al., 2019; Swadener, 2000). The term "students at-promise" is a strength-based label instead of a deficit-based one that stigmatizes students (Dix et al., 2020; C. Robinson, 2017; Samuels, 2020). Shifting from a deficit term to a strength-based term is not the solution for increasing student success among these students. Still, it may contribute positively to how teachers and administrators view them. Additionally, although I am using the term "at-promise," it does not eliminate or change the fact that this population is at risk for failure and dropping out of school for many reasons.

Almost any student may be at-promise under the right circumstances. For this book, I have chosen the definition provided by Stormont and Thomas (2014; see p. 5, Figure 1.1) to describe the risk factors for students at-promise:

> Students who are at risk for failure [or dropping out of school] include students who have within [person] and/or within environmental circumstances that put them in vulnerable positions for having problems in school. These problems can be academic or social or both. Within-person risk factors include [but are not limited to] ADHD, no or limited knowledge/skills or [social, emotional, and behavior problems]. [Some examples of] environmental risks include poverty–homelessness, limited support for learning, [gangs, drugs,] and negative interactions at school, home, or between school and home. (p. 3)

But it is important to keep in mind that being at risk of failure or dropping out does not mean students are bound to fail or drop out.

Common characteristics of students at-promise include low self-confidence with schoolwork, avoidance of school, distrust of adults, and limited notions of their academic future. They often present behavioral problems in the classroom that disrupt the learning process for themselves and others. Many teachers describe these students as burdens in the classroom and feel hopeless in trying to teach them successfully.

Students at-promise often have fragile home lives and may drop out or be forced out of the educational system because of various life circumstances. A majority of students at-promise live in low-income households, meaning they have limited resources, social capital, and parental guidance. They often live in poor, dilapidated neighborhoods plagued with crime and violence. Reduced levels of supervision increase the likelihood of their involvement in negative activities that promote their disconnection from classes and loss of interest in school. They are discouraged learners who view success in school as a matter of luck rather than of their intellect and hard work. Conversely, these students may be pushed out because of age, lack of credit transfer between school districts and states, and differences in educational systems between countries.

We must also keep in mind that students within this population are at-promise for a variety of reasons. They are not a homogeneous group just because they are all at risk of dropping out of school. Some students are at-promise because they have substance abuse problems. Some are bullied. Others are homeless or abused at home. Some work over 40 hours a week in addition to attending school. In other words, a student at-promise can be a student who is the son or daughter of a two-parent, upper-middle-class, professional household or the son or daughter of a poverty-stricken single parent.

Consider these two former students of mine. One student came from a two-parent household. Although both of her parents had college educations and were employed, she was completely disengaged from school, feeling it was a waste of time because school was extremely boring. She failed and dropped out. The other student grew up very poor. He lived with his grandmother rather than with either of his parents. He found it difficult to balance school with his responsibilities at home. To complicate things further, he became a teenage father and eventually dropped out of school. These were two very different scenarios with the same unfortunate result: dropping out. Thus, despite their commonality of being at risk of dropping out of school, students at-promise are in that position for a variety of personal and environmental reasons.

As teachers, we must remember that students at-promise are people before they are students. Only by accepting this first can we expect to work with this population of students effectively. The life experiences these students have outside of school and the problems they face daily, which we often disregard as irrelevant to the classroom, permeate their success in the classroom. Lacking family members or loved ones with education or with real-life examples of people with degrees makes envisioning success in school difficult for students at-promise. They struggle to see school as an arena for improving their lives. School is a long-term investment, but their economic needs are immediate and cannot wait until later to be resolved. Because of their economic needs, students at-promise may view education as an obstacle or a waste of time. The issues of violence, gangs, drugs, and overall danger that surround or engulf students at-promise also detract from students' undivided attention to schoolwork, both in and out of the classroom.

As working professionals, we know that major obstacles within our personal lives impact our performance and ability to succeed in our careers. Why then do we often expect students at-promise to be different? Why do we believe their personal lives outside of school should not hinder their ability to succeed in school? Only when we begin to understand the issues our students face can we incorporate what we have learned into meaningful solutions in the classroom to empower our students through education.

According to the National Center for Education Statistics (NCES), only 85.3 percent of all high school students graduate (NCES, 2019). For community college students, "even after having been in school for six years, fewer than 40% have graduated or transferred to a university," and in universities, 40 percent of all college freshmen never make it to commencement (Kirp, 2019, p. 4). High school dropouts' "median weekly earnings are $606, compared with $749 for high school graduates (no college), $874 for some college or an associate's degree, [and] $1,281 for workers with a bachelor's degree (and no additional degree)" (U.S. Bureau of Labor Statistics, 2019). This income disparity remains constant for many high school and college dropouts throughout their lifetimes and contributes to the ongoing cycle of poverty among the children of high school dropouts.

Increasing the success of students at-promise by enabling them to graduate high school or college will have profound effects not only for the individual students but also for society in general. We will benefit from reductions in the poverty rate, the increased numbers of educated Americans, and the potential economic benefit based on increased numbers of capable, educated workers. To make any of this feasible, however, we must emphasize and teach educators applicable approaches to build meaningful teacher–student relationships within our educational system.

The Researcher

In developing PRT, I worked with dropouts who had been accepted into the Michigan State University High School Equivalency Program (MSU HEP). My background is relatively similar to that of many of the students in that program. I grew up within the feminization of deep poverty in this country. I lived engulfed in the street thug lifestyle and was involved with gangs as a youth. I was labeled a student at-promise throughout school and dropped out of school multiple times. I continued my education at a community college, earning an associate's degree in liberal arts, and transferred to finish my bachelor's degree in sociology. I then went on to earn a master's degree and PhD in sociology.

I am not just an academic writing a book on an alternative pedagogy but a former student at-promise who was supposed to be in prison, dead, or a part of any other statistic within our dropout epidemic. I spent the majority of my life as a young man detesting school, especially the teachers, whom I felt were my enemies. I was so entrenched in my views of school that I categorized all teachers as bad, even before I ever encountered them. I did not allow them the opportunity to get to know me—or teach me—the material I was supposed to learn. I took pride in my rejection of school and in the teachers' inability to connect with me. Disturbing class was entertaining to me. More important, when I was forced to be in school, I simply did nothing. I accepted that I would fail because it was more important for me to resist the teacher and reject the teacher's attempts to teach me. Ultimately, I exercised my only form of power in the classroom as a student: resisting the teacher at the expense of my own success.

In middle school, I specifically remember a teacher who told me one day that whenever I showed up to her class, I ruined her day. I was a talkative young man in her class, I admit—but I did not deserve such a spiteful comment, especially from a teacher. It was at that moment that I decided to resist every single thing she would attempt with me to make her feel the disrespect she made me feel. I never brought paper or pencil to her class whenever I attended. I was constantly disruptive, pushing her beyond her limits. She reached her breaking point one day and simply gave me a paper and told me to draw on it. I told her I didn't have something to write with. She responded, "I do not care! Even if you have to write with your blood, you will find something to write with!" I smiled at her and said okay. As she began teaching the class, I cut my finger with my key and wrote my name on the paper in blood. I raised my hand and asked her to come over. "Is this okay?" I asked. I remember how she gasped, eyes nearly exploding. Her face turned a pasty pale complexion, and her body shook as she told me to get out of her class. I remember how good I felt because my sole purpose in that class was to resist her and to make things impossible for her. My extreme actions were a direct result of her comment. I felt most empowered when I resisted and tortured her, even though it was to my detriment. Such problems, which have existed in classrooms for decades, persist in classes today.

Because I have lived through this and been surrounded by countless others who did as well, creating something to help empower teachers in teaching their most challenging students has become my life's passion. I have always felt strongly that the most powerful person in the classroom is the teacher and that, if teachers are taught effective approaches to apply in their classrooms, they can transform the lives of their students in a positive manner. Fusing my academic knowledge as an educator with my own personal insights as the student no teacher could reach, I have created an authentic approach that will resonate with both teachers and students at-promise in the classroom.

When I was offered the opportunity to work with students in MSU HEP, I was determined to create and implement an alternative teaching pedagogy to help those students pass their general equivalency diploma (GED) examination. Throughout this second edition, you will see examples from the work I did with the MSU HEP students. Additionally, I am providing examples of teachers I have worked with from around the country who have applied PRT in their classrooms. I have continued to refine and implement PRT and to train other teachers in implementing it successfully in their classrooms and schools.

The Pedagogy

A major component within PRT is the concept of Real Talk, an instructor-led discussion surrounding a series of broad, engaging universal themes designed to motivate student-oriented outcomes and to establish connections, understanding, trust, empathy, and caring for one another. In addition to Real Talk, alternative lessons are an important component within PRT. Alternative lessons combine content standard(s) from the curriculum with students' terministic screens (Winterowd, 1985) or external societal issues connected with students' terministic screens. Defining these concepts helps familiarize you with them but does not highlight the complexity of applying them with students. Thus, to help you understand how to conduct and implement these concepts effectively, I will discuss what you must be willing to do with examples from myself and other teachers in Chapter 3.

These concepts alone have utility; as the foundation of this approach, however, it is the combination with other components that makes it distinct and successful. This unique and more encompassing foundation is a combination of the theories of Paulo Freire, Margo Mastropieri and Thomas Scruggs, and Joan Meyer, along with my work with students at-promise. As the core of this pedagogy, Real Talk establishes connections between teachers and students, dismantling the barriers between students at-promise and teachers that inhibit the learning process. This approach is based on five main concepts: (1) relating to and connecting with students, (2) understanding students' personal perspectives, (3) creating an engaging, relevant, and inclusive curriculum for students (4) creating and maintaining a flexible framework in one's teaching strategies, and (5) upholding one's willingness and eagerness to work with students. However, the ability to relate to students is a skill that is not easily taught. Only through actual face-to-face or virtual interactions with students on a consistent basis can teachers establish relatedness.

In preparing to work with students at-promise, establishing an environment of open communication from the first day is critical. In such an environment, teachers gain unique insight into students. Being an active listener allows teachers to relate better to students and to create an engaging, exciting, worthwhile classroom environment. By *active listening*, I refer to an explicit effort not only to hear the words of students but also to listen to the entire message they are trying to convey. Incorporating active listening with students can be achieved by implementing a few simple steps:

- Look at them directly; they must have your undivided attention (no multitasking).
- Pay attention to their body language.
- Use your body language to show them you are listening (e.g., nodding your head occasionally, smiling when appropriate,

offering small comments like "uh-huh" or "yes" to encourage them to continue speaking).

- Do not interrupt them as they are trying to make their point. Foster genuine communication with students, allowing them to teach you about their perspectives, realities, worldviews, and experiences.

With this information, I developed lectures, lessons, and assignments focused on their experiences. The HEP students were extremely receptive to my pedagogy because the material covered in class was directly related to their lives. However, this alone did not guarantee they would pass the GED.

I continued to refine my approach by ensuring that all class activities were inclusive and integrated the core concepts of the curriculum. The students became more engaged in class and receptive to learning. Because they needed to develop a deeper understanding of the concepts related to the GED exam, I focused on integrating those concepts into Real Talk. Providing a consistent classroom structure throughout the semester was also crucial to the students' success.

In the following chapter, I explain PRT more fully. We will explore the theoretical foundations of the pedagogy, see how various aspects of the pedagogy were implemented, and learn how to implement PRT in any classroom with any subject matter.

If you have been looking for ways to reach your students at-promise, help them succeed, and find tools with which to sharpen your teaching continually, read on. The approach can be used by first-year teachers, 30-year veterans, and anyone in between. Teachers of all backgrounds, racial groups, gender, sexuality, and social classes can use this approach with any population of students at-promise. The focus of this pedagogy is not the teacher or the teacher's background; it is the connections established with the students, regardless of background. It is about maximizing connections through universal emotions that are not necessarily focused specifically on life experiences alone. PRT will give you the framework and strategies to succeed.

Note

1. The feminization of deep poverty refers to the disproportionate percentage of households headed by single females living 50 percent below the poverty level.

PRT 2

Teaching through methods and strategies that build better connections with students improves their academic performance. That's what PRT is all about. The word "pedagogy" comes from the Greek roots *pais* ("child") and *ago* ("to lead"), meaning "to lead a child." In education, the term refers to specific approaches used by teachers to transmit knowledge to students, usually through structured curricula. The pedagogy that teachers choose becomes the basis for designing and implementing lessons, in-class assignments, homework, study guides, reviews, and other exercises to help their students learn the expected curriculum content. The specific approach chosen by the teacher also dictates the type of relationship created between the teacher and the student. By creating inclusive, structured, student-oriented learning environments, teachers can achieve success with their students at-promise.

The Theoretical Foundations of Real Talk

PRT is a teaching approach founded on a combination of three existing models of education, extracting concepts from the work of Paulo Freire (1970) on liberation education, of Margo Mastropieri and Thomas Scruggs (2001) on promoting inclusion in the classroom, and of Joan Meyer (1968) on characteristics of successful teachers. Doing so maximized the strengths of each approach because they complement each other. The work was strengthened further by the additional concepts I integrated. Thus, PRT encompasses more than any individual model.

In the following sections, each of the contributions from these models is further examined: dialogue (Freire), S.C.R.E.A.M. (Mastropieri and Scruggs), and the characteristics of successful teachers (Meyer).

Dialogue

In *Pedagogy of the Oppressed* (1970), a book dedicated to the poor of Brazil, Freire offered a major pedagogical approach for teachers to use in working with disadvantaged populations. Emphasizing the concept of dialogue, this model fosters teachers and students learning from one another. By integrating students' input and perspectives in the learning process, teachers make lessons more relevant to students' lives while encouraging them to become an intricate part of the classroom. In doing so, teachers recognize and affirm students' voices, resulting in an environment in which students and teachers grow together.

Freire focused on "the fundamental goal of dialogical teaching" in which learning and knowing "involve theorizing about experiences shared in the dialogue" (Macedo, 2000, p. 17). In this liberation education model, teachers take a role with their students in relating to their students' perspectives and lives. Rather than the traditional roles within classrooms of "teacher of the students and students of the teacher" (Freire, 1970, p. 80), both teachers and students are teachers and students. In Freire's terminology, they become "teacher–student with students–teachers" (Freire, 1970, p. 80). As such, both teachers and students have responsibility for the process, allowing each person to grow.

Teachers must develop learning environments dedicated to the lives of students at-promise by connecting their life experiences to learning. Teachers begin this process by learning about their students through the established dialogue. As the teachers learn about their students' lives and the things that are pertinent to them, teachers can teach in a manner that is relevant to their students' lives. Instead of using a strict approach to curriculum that is not effective with the oppressed (i.e., students at-promise), teachers base lessons and lectures on the experiences and lives of their students.

This dialogue is also the basis for Freire's problem-posing approach through which teachers use the reflections of their students to reform their own reflections. Through dialogue with their teachers, students become critical investigators, creating a continuous state of interaction and active listening. Thus, classrooms become places that foster critical development. As teachers pose problems related to their students and their world, they challenge students to respond. With such problems, students begin to see interrelationships within the context of the world in which they live rather than irrelevant information. With each problem, their comprehension becomes more critical.

Students at-promise maintain their engagement as they learn the subjects and concepts being taught because with each new challenge, they develop new understandings. In turn, their responses lead to new challenges. Through the dialogue process, then, students feel "less alienated" (Freire, 1970, p. 81) and become committed to learning in their classrooms. Unfortunately, many educators within the United States have adapted this pedagogy into a methodological approach rather than using the dialogue Freire intended.

S.C.R.E.A.M.

To build inclusive classrooms and work with students at-promise, Mastropieri and Scruggs (2018, pp. 136–140) identified six variables teachers should include to provoke more engaged and active student involvement in the classroom and throughout the learning process. These six variables are structure (S), clarity (C), redundancy (R), enthusiasm (E), appropriate pace (A), and maximized engagement (M), collectively known as S.C.R.E.A.M. In incorporating S.C.R.E.A.M. into PRT, there is expansion of some sections for further clarification. Teachers should analyze their classes to determine which of the six variables they are incorporating and how effectively they are doing so. In this way, teachers can identify their classroom strengths and any areas they should develop more fully.

Structure

This component concerns setting up the classroom with the students. Teachers must ensure that they use appropriate curriculum and that they target students' learning styles. Students should know and understand the short- and long-term goals of the class and how their teachers can assist them in achieving these goals.

Clarity

Clarity is imperative to ensure that (a) students understand their teachers' expectations of their students and that (b) teachers understand their students' expectations of their teachers. Teachers should avoid making assumptions about what students know or do not know. Incorporating this variable will greatly reduce misunderstandings and misinterpretations within classrooms.

Redundancy

This component concerns teachers teaching subject matter in a variety of ways and allowing students to practice concepts and subject matter in diverse ways. Redundancy includes repetition, reiteration, diverse explanations and examples, and reinforcement. This in turn allows teachers to specifically address the diverse learning styles of their students.

Enthusiasm

This component is essential for teachers in working with students at-promise. Teachers should show their enthusiasm daily throughout each class period, but this must be done in an authentic, nonsuperficial manner. If done superficially, this population of students will notice immediately, costing teachers their credibility and the opportunity to connect with their students. Teachers must show genuine enthusiasm in presenting new material and in reviewing previously introduced material. Enthusiasm does not mean pretending to be happy; it means being fervent in teaching the material to your students. We must remain positive when teaching. When we have difficult days, as do all human beings, we must be willing to be genuine about our struggles yet remain positive toward our students' success.

Appropriate Pace

Teachers must carefully determine the appropriate pace by considering student needs and learning as the class progresses. Teachers must constantly analyze and reflect on what is occurring in their classrooms to determine if the pace needs to be increased or decreased to maximize student learning. By employing a needs-based pace, teachers will help students feel that they can keep up with the teacher as they learn the material and increase their comfort level in the classroom.

In today's classrooms, teachers must teach toward state-imposed standards. Teachers must keep students on a pace that will allow them to address all of the standards within their subject areas. This can prove to be very difficult for some teachers. By taking the time to determine the appropriate pace for the class, teachers will be able to decipher what is slowing students down. Teachers can then address these issues and move the class at a brisker, more homogenous pace to achieve the necessary standards or goals.

Maximized Engagement

This is the final component teachers should employ to support student engagement in classrooms at-promise. In maximizing engagement, teachers make sure every student is involved at some level with what is occurring in their classroom. For example, to engage students in a lecture, ensure they are active listeners. Allow students to ask questions during the lecture. Ask for student input on the subject matter. Ask for help with distributing papers or with logistical matters in the classroom. In other words, allow students to become an intricate part of the classroom. By doing so, teachers give students a sense of worth and belonging because they are engaged in classroom matters on a day-to-day basis.

Characteristics of Successful Teachers

The final piece of the theoretical foundation for Real Talk is the characteristics of successful teachers as defined by Joan Meyer (1968). She found three characteristics that determine a teacher's success with students at-promise: (1) the ability to relate to students personally, (2) the ability to teach the students, and (3) the teacher's attitude toward the students. In relating to students, successful teachers incorporate student-centered approaches to their teaching and develop insight into their students. Such teachers are personally flexible and routinely engage in critical self-evaluation. In addition, they are willing to listen to their students and counsel them whenever needed. An important thing to remember is that we do not have to have the same experiences as our students to be able to relate with them. We must only be willing to attempt to connect with them. This allows us to relate to our students even when at first glance they may seem very different from us.

Successful teachers are flexible and creative. They are dynamic. They are willingly go beyond the minimum efforts required and invest their energy into their students. They try new and different things to find successful approaches to improve their students' passing rates. Successful teachers approach their students as people, not just as their teachers. They encourage personal interactions with their students and show through their actions that they are "positive, accepting, and caring" (Meyer, 1968).

Meyer's characteristics are an important aspect of my pedagogy. Teachers who have these qualities most easily adapt and successfully use the aspects combined within my approach. PRT is not about finding the most successful teachers or those struggling the most; it is about finding the teachers who are receptive to trying something new in the classroom. After all, PRT will not work if we are not willing to try it or to admit that we all have room for improvement within our lives. Meyer's characteristics within my approach give us an important step in finding new levels of success in working with students at-promise.

Refinement of PRT

Combining aspects extracted from Freire's dialogue, Mastropieri and Scruggs's S.C.R.E.A.M. variables, and Meyer's characteristics of successful teachers, I developed the unique foundation of PRT. To these three education models, sociological theory was adopted as a lens through which teachers can better understand their students. Additionally, four concepts were added to strengthen PRT:

(1) terministic screen, (2) alternative lessons (3) flexibility, and (4) Real Talk discussions.

Symbolic Interactionism

To understand the perspectives of students, Herbert Blumer's (1969) sociological theory of symbolic interactionism (SI) was used. Blumer based this theory on the fact that humans create and use symbols. Symbolic interactionism rests on three simple premises:

1. Humans beings act toward things on the basis of the meaning that things have for them.

2. The meaning of such things is derived from, or arises out of, the social interaction that one has with one's fellows.

3. These meanings are handled in, and modified through, an interpretive process used by the person in dealing with the things he encounters. (Blumer, 1969, p. 2)

In other words, human beings respond, interact, and react to the meaning that things have for them; moreover, that meaning is created based on how other people respond to them regarding this meaning.

SI is crucial to PRT. Before we can begin to understand the complexities of student learning in our schools, we must first understand that we live in a society that is socially constructed. *Social construction* means "people behave on what they believe, not just what is objectively true. Thus, society is considered to be socially constructed through human interpretation" (Anderson & Taylor, 2012, p. 16). Understanding this social construction is the first step in seeing clearly that students are not merely students. They are people before they are students—people with diverse views and understandings of the society in which they live. Students at-promise do not displace these views when they step into classrooms. Their perspectives permeate their classrooms. The same is true for educators. Their socially constructed views also infuse the classroom. Understanding and accepting this theoretical foundation is the first step in creating a foundation built on understanding that, in the classroom, the view of the teacher is not the only way to view the world; students also have their views and interpretations.

Students hold multiple identities within their lives, just as every single one of us does. In no particular order, I am a professor, a son, a brother, a cousin, an uncle, a board member, and so on. Although I am the same person, I play different roles within each identity I hold within my life and society. These things influence my social construction of reality. It is no different for our students. In the classroom, they are our students. Outside of the classroom but within the school boundaries, they may be jocks, gang members, thugs, or any other cultural style that is in vogue. Outside of school, they may be sons, daughters, fathers, mothers, leaders of groups, employees, and so on. Just like us, they are impacted by these identities. Once we understand this reality, we can begin the process of effectively teaching our students.

Comprehending and accepting that a teacher's reality may differ drastically from a student at-promise is the first step in overcoming barriers between the two groups. For example, a teacher's reality may include owning a home and donating money to a local homeless shelter. A student at-promise may have a reality wherein they have no home at all and wait in line at the local homeless shelter nightly to eat dinner. SI helps us understand that people who live within the same society and the same relative area may have quite different realities.

SI is not an applicable, tangible tool we can use in the classroom; rather, it is a perspective through which we work within our classrooms. This perspective begins before we ever enter our classrooms to teach. We must truly view and respect our students as people whose views are socially constructed. Through this view, we can begin the teaching process with open minds rather than the more traditional mindset of imposing our views as teacher onto our students at-promise through the educational process. By understanding the SI approach at its most basic level, we can begin teaching in a transformative manner rather than in a potentially alienating or oppressive way.

By accepting the SI perspective, we can begin to understand how people make sense of the world. We can then create a dialogue with our students, communicating with them in a manner to which they are receptive. We can also focus on our students' school experiences, analyzing them to provide insight into how they communicate and how we interpret each other's perspectives.

Terministic Screens

Kenneth Burke defined "terministic screen" as the way in which individuals view the world (Winterowd, 1985). Individuals form their views, which are reflected in their perspectives, based on their group memberships and ascribed or achieved status as individuals within society. Thus, terministic screens are heavily influenced by an individual's group memberships (e.g., social class, race, gender, sexuality, education, political affiliation).

Rockler (2002) described this concept as a way to deepen one's understanding of how people view the world around them. He used Burke's example of comparing terministic screens to the color filters photographers use. Each filter allows different aspects on the picture to be seen more clearly, each revealing different truths about the object or scene being depicted. Thus, something that seems factual or true when observed through one filter may reveal an entirely different understanding when viewed through a different filter.

Terministic screens also affect the vocabulary we use. We usually try to use words that reflect reality. However, our words are actually reflections of our perceptions of reality. In seeing one aspect of reality, we deflect another. Thus, one person's reality may not be the same as another person's because of our individual terministic screens. In other words, when two people see or experience the same thing, they may not perceive the experience the same way because of their filters. What may be wonderfully clear to one person can be muddled confusion to another. What one person sees as beautiful, another sees as plain, ugly, or obscene. Thus, two people in a conversation may draw very different meanings from what is said. Ultimately, terministic screens affect how we view and interpret the world. In PRT, educators examine each student's terministic screen to create meaningful, relevant curriculum and learning environments, inclusive of each student's learning needs.

Teachers can also understand their own perspectives better. In trying to understand their students, teachers must attempt to determine and understand their terministic screens. As a result, no longer will students simply listen to the teacher; they will also engage with their teachers in building effective pedagogy.

Alternative Lessons

The second concept, alternative lessons, is defined in Chapter 1 as the combination of content standard(s) from the curriculum with students' terministic screens or external societal issues connected with students' terministic screens. Alternative lessons make your classroom inclusive, engaging, and relevant for students and are vital to PRT. Unlike Real Talk, alternative lessons can happen every day, but they take time and effort to create. Once created, alternative lessons become part of your everyday classroom teaching and eventually transform the curriculum's content and delivery.

Many teachers have raised a common question over the years: What is the difference between an alternative lesson and active learning (e.g., classroom discussion, think-pair-share, collaborative group work, etc.)? Active learning falls within alternative lessons. Active learning lessons that use students' terministic screens or connect societal issues outside the classroom that resonate with students' terministic screens are alternative lessons. There are many ways to conduct alternative lessons. The most important requirement for alternative lessons is to embed students' terministic screens. One of my favorite descriptions of how powerful alternative lessons are in the classroom came from a teacher who said, "Alternative lessons remove the fear of learning for my students and insert their experience within the curriculum."

Because creative teachers have designed and implemented alternative lessons in their classrooms, alternative lessons have taken shape in many unique ways. For example, a history teacher and an English teacher collaborated to create an alternative lesson for their classes. They decided to focus on their students' personal histories and U.S. history. The teachers asked students to make one-minute videos describing something specific about their personal history and U.S. history they considered important and why it was important to them. After students submitted their videos, they wrote about their experiences creating the videos and shared what they learned about themselves and their U.S. history topic.

In another example, a math teacher created an alternative lesson to represent his students better. This teacher noticed that the number of students of color in his class was increasing over time. As this teacher and I worked together, he realized his curriculum did not represent his students. To remedy this problem, the teacher created an alternative lesson focused on the struggle to raise capital, secure loans, or grants to grow small businesses owned by people of color, ultimately showing how success can happen despite the challenges. Using YouTube videos highlighting small businesses owned by different people of color in varied industries, he managed to connect everything back to his math class and teach students the curriculum's necessary concepts. The positive feedback this teacher received from his students of color was a wonderful experience for him. Students shared how much they appreciated learning about math through seeing, hearing, and discussing businesses owned by people of color. Students also shared they felt a connection to the math class they had never felt in other math classes. The result of this alternative lesson was a transformative experience for the students and teacher alike.

A final example is an alternative lesson I created for my students based on a professional boxer. I have used this alternative lesson in many different ways, but I will focus on stereotypes and biases in this example. Based on what I learned from my students, social media and social media influencers play an important role in many of their lives. With this in mind, I created my alternative lesson, "A Future Star" (Hernandez & Loebick, 2016), to teach students about stereotypes and biases while also challenging their existing stereotypes and biases. Through an interactive presentation, I shared information and posed questions to my students to encourage them to share their perspectives.

In the first bullet on the first slide, I share the boxer's fight record, followed by the second bullet that states, "pictures of a future star." I immediately follow by showing students different pictures of the boxer. The pictures show a young man in "great physical shape. His face is freckled, his hair and eyebrows are bright red, and his eyes are brown." Once my students have seen the pictures, I ask, "How can we promote him to maximize his earning potential." After sharing their ideas, ranging from nicknames, marketing plans, and social media platforms, I show them a YouTube clip that shows the boxer speaking Spanish. The most common response from my students is confusion. Typically, students did not expect the white, red-headed boxer to speak fluent Spanish. The final PowerPoint slide I show informs students that the boxer is Latino, specifically Mexican, born and raised in the Mexican state of Jalisco. This understanding leads the class to discuss, "What do Latinos look like?" This alternative lesson about an important topic students often disengage from or are uncomfortable discussing has been a powerful experience for many of my students.

Alternative lessons take time and effort to create and are not always immediately effective. For example, a teacher once shared with me that his alternative lesson was successful in two of his classes, but when he tried the same lesson in a third class, it did not go well. It takes practice and learning to conduct alternative lessons effectively with various student audiences. As you create and implement more alternative lessons in your classes, you will continually make changes to become comfortable with their effectiveness. As you build a stock of alternative lessons, some may be timeless, while others will need updating to meet your students where they are. As you progress with creating alternative lessons, they will become a part of preparing to teach your classes. Alternative lessons will eventually become a seamless and natural part of the teaching process for you.

Flexibility

The third concept, flexibility, is added to the S.C.R.E.A.M. variables. Flexibility is the teacher's ability to incorporate every aspect of S.C.R.E.A.M. across multiple classes with a variety of students while always maintaining the possibility for change. With flexibility, teachers can adapt core concepts to the unique needs of all students and achieve consistent results over time with different sets of students.

Too often as educators, we allow rigidity to overtake our approach to teaching, making it difficult for us to part with comfortable teaching routines. Maintaining the status quo may seem to make teaching easier, but ultimately, it does not fully benefit our students. We need to grow continually as teachers, learning new information to build a flexible repertoire of lessons, lectures, classroom assignments, and homework. With flexibility, we can foster environments inclusive of all our students' unique needs and learning characteristics.

Real Talk Discussions

The last concept and the most powerful component of the pedagogy is Real Talk discussions. Real Talks are instructor-led discussions based on a series of broad, engaging universal themes to motivate student-oriented outcomes. Real Talk is a systematic yet authentic approach to establishing understanding, trust, empathy, and caring for one another through which teachers can establish powerful, genuine connections with their students or between their students and the established curriculum.

Universal themes can be quite diverse. For example, themes tied to experiences with happiness, anger, motivation, frustration, sadness, excitement, bitterness, or confusion can be used to generate Real Talk discussions. However, these are just examples, and no teacher should feel limited to these themes. The point of universal themes is that everyone can relate to them at some level or another. Regardless of social class, race, gender, sexuality, level of education, or unique experiences, we all have common human needs or emotions that we share. Thus, teachers should identify Real Talk themes that resonate or connect not only with themselves but also with their students.

To give a more vivid explanation of how to use Real Talk in the classroom, we must imagine a funnel. We pick a theme such as adversity and begin at the top of the funnel. If necessary, we define "adversity" and make sure everyone in class knows what it means. As we proceed further down the funnel, we connect adversity to ourselves (the teacher). We explain how we know adversity and how we've experienced it or how friends, family, or loved ones have experienced adversity.

The best and most powerful examples are those from our own lives or the lives of friends, family members, and loved ones. However, if we don't have any examples that are applicable to the theme or if we are uncomfortable sharing our experiences, we can pull examples from other sources, such as autobiographies, documentaries, music lyrics, or current news stories. I must stress, however, how powerful our own personal examples are. Therefore, teachers who find it difficult to engage in Real Talk because it is uncomfortable or scary or who are unwilling to try this approach should speak with teachers who are using Real Talk successfully. Don't give up on the approach before giving it a fair chance.

After connecting the theme (i.e., adversity) with ourselves, we move further down the funnel, transitioning to our students by asking them about their experiences with adversity: How do they know adversity within their own lives? How have they experienced it? If they are shy or unwilling to discuss their personal experiences, ask them how their friends, family, or loved ones have experienced adversity. It is at this juncture that we begin to make connections with our students, allowing them to share and connect with us in the classroom. We may not get immediate jumping-out-of-seats, anxious-to-be-involved reactions during the first few Real Talks, but we will notice a change in the demeanor and atmosphere of the class. Slowly but surely, we will have one or two students raise their hands and share something regarding adversity within their lives. Those not sharing openly may be engaging in self-reflection or nodding in agreement, indicating they relate to the questions.

Continuing down the funnel, we begin to connect the Real Talk discussion to the classroom. We have multiple ways to do this. Through Real Talk, we establish and deepen our connections with students. We can also inspire, refocus, or encourage our classes. Additionally, we can use Real Talk to help our students become receptive to concepts, lessons, chapters, or anything else they must learn in class that they usually resist or find intimidating.

I once used pain as a theme and shared a negative and unfortunate experience I had had in school on Valentine's Day. I also shared how, in the long run, that experience had motivated me throughout my life. I used this specific story with my students shortly after they had experienced racial attacks at the university. I wanted to reengage them rather than lose them to the rage they were feeling as victims of racial discrimination. Through the Real Talk focused on my Valentine's Day experience, I turned the students' anger into something more productive, redirecting it to their schoolwork.

Real Talk allows us to connect with students, build rapport, and gain insight to their terministic screens. Even though the most powerful person in the classroom is the teacher, students have their own form of power: the power to resist teachers and their attempts to engage their students. Through Real Talk, we can make meaningful connections with our students, especially in classrooms where we may be having difficulty in establishing connections. Helping our students become receptive, in turn, allows us to teach them.

Real Talk also helps to dispel the common notion many students have that teachers only exist in the classroom. Students who see their teachers outside the classroom are often disbelieving, saying such things as "Mrs. Smith? What are you doing here?" when they see her at the grocery store. It does not occur to them, as they see Mrs. Smith holding a jar of peanut butter, that she's out of food at home and, like the students or their parents, has come to the supermarket to buy groceries. Such incidents should show us that our students do not view us as people but as teachers. It's as if, when the students leave their classrooms, they believe we stand up, walk to a corner, and plug ourselves into a power outlet to recharge because the next day our students see us in the same classroom settings we were in the day before. Real Talk helps us dismantle this idea, showing our students that we are persons before we are teachers.

This phenomenon works in reverse as well. Seeing our students outside of class can give us entirely different perspectives about who they are. Through Real Talk, we can begin to see the complex people sitting in front of us rather than merely groups of students. Thus, Real Talk is an extremely valuable tool in helping us overcome the barriers between students at-promise and us, their teachers. Such barriers, which are otherwise seldom overcome, hinder the teaching and learning that is supposed to take place in our classrooms.

Strategic Placement of Real Talk

Teachers need time and practice to become comfortable enough with Real Talk to use it effectively in their classrooms. It is not a technique that can be "winged." Practice does not mean preparing note cards as one does for formal presentations. Rather, it means feeling comfortable with engaging students in Real Talk within the classroom. This involves being authentic yet structured enough that each Real Talk discussion has a clear purpose and a point that connects with their students. As teachers become more comfortable with Real Talk and more advanced in using it within their classrooms, they will begin to recognize teachable moments in their classrooms when they can connect to a Real Talk on the spot. They will also find their students initiating Real Talks, giving teachers another avenue to contribute in a meaningful manner.

Real Talk is not something teachers should use every day. Doing so will diminish the significance of these talks. Teachers who have been trained in Real Talk and have applied it in their classrooms have constantly heard their students ask, "When will you do one of your special talks again?" We keep students on the edge of their seats by delving into strategically placed Real Talks.

Teachers should follow a general time frame in implementing Real Talks, placing them periodically throughout the duration of their courses. Strategically embedding three different Real Talk discussions over the semester is ideal. The first interaction with students is crucial to establish connections or, at the very least, a neutral setting that can lead to positive relationships. The first Real Talk can be planned for the first day of class to captivate students and "hook" them with the first interaction. Using Real Talk on the first day to captivate our students and introduce ourselves to our classes will set the tone for the semester. However, because it takes time to feel comfortable delivering a Real Talk, teachers who are not comfortable using it on the first day of class should aim for one sometime during the first week of classes.

The second Real Talk should be scheduled halfway through the course. Every teacher knows that there is a point in the middle of the semester when students exponentially begin struggling to stay focused and to do their work. Midsemester is a crucial time. If we do not act to meet their need for reinvigoration and focus, we can lose our students. An appropriate Real Talk at this point can provide just the inspiration needed to refocus and reenergize both our students and ourselves. How we tie in Real Talks at this point is ultimately at our individual discretion, based on our students, our subject matter, and ourselves. What works in one teacher's class may not be the right Real Talk for anyone else's, but if it meets the needs of our students, it's the right Real Talk to stimulate our students' attention.

The final preplanned Real Talk of the semester should occur near the end of the course, at some point one or two weeks before final exams. Because teachers know their students well by this time, including their specific needs, they will know best when to schedule this last Real Talk. Students are often "burned out" at this point in the semester. Therefore, the purpose of this final Real Talk should be an uplifting catalyst for students to end the semester in a strong fashion, both in terms of their final exams and their overall work in the class.

Ultimately, the decision about when and how often to use Real Talks is up to each teacher. The foundational placement suggested may be sufficient for many teachers. Others may find that having Real Talks once a month or using Real Talks to introduce specific lessons, concepts, or chapters that are difficult for students to grasp will be the best way to engage their students. Some teachers may also become comfortable enough to use Real Talks sporadically when they encounter those "teachable moments," opportunities to connect with their students in terms of a particular concept or to develop rapport. However, it is essential that teachers not overuse Real Talk during a course. Overuse will diminish the power and influence of Real Talk.

PRT and Other Approaches

In most pedagogies, teachers are expected to give the required information to students. This may be done in various ways, including lectures, videos, texts, activities, and exercises. Some pedagogies will also ask teachers to get to know their students or perhaps to understand "where their students come from" to be more effective when teaching them. Seldom, however, are teachers given a step-by-step approach on how to connect or get to know their students. Thus, in most approaches, teaching ultimately involves one-way communication: The teacher teaches; the students learn. Real Talk is different. It is a two-way process. Not only does the teacher teach the students, but the students also teach the teacher. When teachers teach their curricula with this pedagogy, they are not using an approach that is exclusively teacher led; nor is it focused simply on filling students with the required information. This two-way teaching process is essential to the success of Real Talk.

In traditional pedagogies, teachers get to know their students mainly through structured, often inflexible processes of formal, systematic observations and ongoing assessments and documentation of learning. In Real Talk, teachers get to know their students through meaningful dialogue as well. Teachers learn about their students from their students: their lives, their perspectives, and their insights. By engaging students as people outside of their roles as students, teachers can structure their classes according to their students' needs and their abilities to relate curricular concepts to their lives. Real Talk allows teachers to establish a systematic yet authentic way to captivate and connect with their students, including their students at-promise, while remaining themselves.

In most traditional pedagogies, teachers are also the solution finders. When something is not working and students are not learning as they should, the teachers are the ones with the responsibility to determine what is wrong. They must find alternatives that will ensure student learning and success. In Real Talk, teachers see their students as resources and use the students' perspectives to find answers to classroom challenges.

PRT is also very flexible in that it does not have to be adopted in its entirety to be used effectively. Teaching is an art form and a science that takes time to master, a process under constant evolution, which must be considered when creating a pedagogical approach for teachers to apply in their classrooms. Many approaches expect teachers to adopt an entirely new pedagogical approach to be effective with challenging students, regardless of any success teachers may have already had with students at-promise.

I acknowledge, credit, and respect the many teachers who have been or are attempting to become successful in working with students at-promise. Those who are achieving success are doing many things correctly, which must be acknowledged. But everyone in society has room to improve what they do within their professions. In this specific case, all educators have room to improve their craft of teaching. For that reason, PRT is unique in that teachers can adapt it to meet their needs in working with students at-promise. Teachers struggling to find success with students at-promise will find adopting the entire approach to be ideal. Teachers already using some of the elements may begin with whatever component fits into their existing classroom structure to enhance the success they are experiencing. This approach is meant to be adaptable, encompassing, and applicable in the classroom no matter how much of it a teacher chooses to use. Whether using the entire approach or selected components to fill gaps in an already successful teaching methodology, teachers simply must be willing to try the approach to see how it can improve their success with students at-promise.

I worked with a first-year white teacher at a predominantly African American urban school. This gentleman was struggling tremendously to connect with his students. He shared that he desperately and wholeheartedly wanted to make genuine connections with his students. Although he was quite receptive to the training and was willing to try the approach, I could sense some hesitation. After a few weeks, he was finally ready to begin implementing the approach in his classroom. The first day he conducted a Real Talk that was nothing short of stellar, as his email to me after this first effort showed:

Dr. Hernandez,

> I wanted to share that my first Real Talk went extremely well! About 90% of my students were absolutely engaged, nodding in agreement, and their eyes fixed on our conversation . . . the most remarkable interaction was how [receptive], respectful, and engaged they were. . . . Students came up to me after class, wanted to know more updates about my demeaning experience, and a few that did not share told me that they "really got" what I was saying.

> . . . I was willing to try your approach, but I have to be honest, as I was not completely sold on the type of powerful impact you said it would have on both my students and [me] . . . I am just blown away with what I have just experienced and want to keep this momentum going. . . . You have made a believer out of me regarding the impact and results of your pedagogy.

What this teacher shared is ultimately what other educators will experience when using PRT in their classrooms. However, PRT takes time. Even though this teacher had tremendous success the first time he used Real Talk in his classroom, results will vary from teacher to teacher. Successful application of this pedagogy, as with any pedagogy, does not happen in an instant; it requires time to learn to apply it correctly and consistently within the classroom. It also requires open-mindedness and a wholehearted approach, amongst other variables discussed in the next chapter.

NOTES

What Must Be True About You 3

Over many years of leading professional development, I eventually came to recognize several essential characteristics that I took for granted yet relied on for effective teaching. Vulnerability, empathy, growth mindset, creativity, and grit play explicit and important roles in PRT as a whole. Although many people have discussed these concepts, I highlight the work of specific thought leaders whose perspectives play a role in my work, including Dr. Brené Brown (vulnerability), Dr. Helen Reiss (empathy), Dr. Carol Dweck (growth mindset), Dr. Ken Robinson and Kevin Ashton (creativity), and Dr. Angela Duckworth (grit). Individually, each concept is essential, but they are most valuable and effective when combined, both in PRT as a whole and when conducting Real Talk and alternative lessons.

The examples I share demonstrate how each concept works within Real Talk, alternative lessons, or both. Keep in mind, as you read the examples, that implementing PRT is possible at any educational level, from K–12 through higher education. I encourage you to focus on extracting the approach described in each example and on considering how you can best adapt it to your classroom.

Vulnerability

The first step to developing and delivering a compelling Real Talk is to ask yourself if you are ready and willing to be authentically vulnerable with your students. For the Real Talk method, vulnerability means "uncertainty, risk, and emotional exposure" (Brown, 2015, p. 34). Each Real Talk must incorporate vulnerability; otherwise, you will inhibit your efforts to connect effectively with students.

I've encountered some teachers who seemed indifferent or disingenuous about their use of vulnerability, despite their best intentions. A history teacher once shared her frustration with Real Talks "falling flat" and ultimately creating more of a barrier between her and her students. Her mistake became obvious to me when I asked her if she was vulnerable during Real Talk. The response was no. I asked why not. She said, "I want them to know very little about me, and I don't want them to know how I feel." Therefore, her Real Talk came off as insincere and disconnected because it was. Her demeanor was rigid, stoic, and forced, which caused students to respond negatively. They struggled to interpret what she was sharing, and they could not connect with her Real Talk. If you want to connect with students, you must be willing to be vulnerable. This is the only way to create an environment in which students will be vulnerable too.

Being vulnerable is no easy task; I resisted it myself throughout my early career, and I still do from time to time. My background and cultural upbringing taught me that vulnerability was a weakness. I wanted to connect with my students, but I did not know how to be vulnerable, which made me feel frustrated and angry. In the classroom, my resistance to vulnerability was projected through my tone of voice. I expressed myself as confident and strong, in a straightforward way and exhibiting my expertise. I mistakenly thought this approach would bring us closer together. I was wrong; it just pushed us further apart, and in many cases, my students were intimidated by me. I was at a loss. I was honest with them, but honesty wasn't helping us connect. I still had a lot to learn about being vulnerable to connect with others.

In graduate school, I had a professor who was a mountain of a man with an even bigger heart. He embraced me from the day I met him. He was kind, generous, wise, committed to equity, and a brilliant scholar. As the years progressed, he became a mentor and friend. One day, after not having seen each other for a while, we bumped into each other in a building. I was walking with my usual intensity and stoic gaze, cutting through a crowd of people. Towering over everyone around us, he yelled, "Paul! Look at you. You look like an NFL linebacker! You look good and healthy! Come see me to catch up." He brought a genuine smile to my face, and I said that I would indeed come and see him.

When we got together, it was as if he knew exactly what I was feeling. After the usual pleasantries, he said something that changed my life: "Paul, you've got that intensity on full blast. I mean, you even intimidate me, and we are friends. You need to let it go; you are limiting yourself in everything you do. Let your guard down and let yourself be seen. It doesn't make you weak; it makes you brave, strong, and human."

His words shook me to my core. As we stood up to say goodbye, instead of our usual handshake and half-hug, he hugged me tightly. That hug allowed me to be vulnerable without feeling weak. It made me feel whole. I felt a massive weight being lifted off my shoulders.

This experience became part of my journey toward embracing vulnerability and putting it into practice through Real Talk in my classroom. It did not happen overnight, but through a reflective and gradual process, I grew more comfortable with vulnerability over time, and it became a part of my teaching. Ultimately, this made my Real Talks effective and powerful.

Without vulnerability, we cannot connect with students. Brown (2015, p. 113) says it beautifully: "The irony is that when we're standing across from someone hidden or shielded by masks and armor, we feel frustrated and disconnected." Students learn more from teachers who allow themselves to be seen as humans rather than as controlling forces hiding behind the curriculum.

No teacher embodies the transformation that comes from embracing vulnerability better than KH. I first met her at a conference for career and technical education, where I was the keynote speaker. Months later, she emailed me to request a meeting to discuss the issues she was facing in her courses.

KH explained that she wanted to increase the retention of her first-year nursing students, especially during the first semester. She explained that first-semester students took an intense, multifaceted course consisting of physical assessment labs, skills labs, medical terminology, medication math, lectures on various topics, and clinicals. To increase student retention, she had begun offering optional support sessions once a week, lasting two hours (although students could come and go at any point during the session) and providing supplemental learning tools. To her surprise, students were not showing up for the extra help, even though she encouraged them to attend.

Rather than becoming angry or disillusioned, KH had the humility and eagerness to seek support to serve her students better. She said she had reached out to me partly because my willingness to be vulnerable in front of people had impressed her. She distinctly remembered how I connected with the audience (including herself) through my vulnerability, and she thought I could help her better connect with and engage her students so they would attend her support sessions. (Interestingly, in this case, my own vulnerability as a keynote speaker had created the connection that would help her solve her struggle.)

I asked KH, "How do you begin teaching in the classroom when you first meet students?" She reflected briefly and then answered, "It's interesting you asked me this because I was recently thinking about it. I tell them who I am; I go on to tell them my professional experience, my credentials, and my schooling. But the last time I did this, I saw their faces drop, and they seemed to be pulling away from me. I realized this might not be the best way to do things. But I had always done this, and I was comfortable doing it this way." This response is consistent with that of many other teachers, who, with some variations, have emphasized that they already share details about themselves with students. However, the type of sharing they describe does not lead to developing a connection with students. To connect with our students and enable them to connect with us, we must break away from the flawed mindset of "I want to experience your vulnerability, but I don't want to be vulnerable" (Brown, 2015, p. 42).

My next question for KH was "Do you ever share your experiences with your students? Do you talk about what you went through to get to where you are today?" She replied, "No, absolutely not. I don't feel comfortable doing that; they don't need to know that stuff." When I asked her why she thought that way, she said, "Because I don't feel comfortable sharing my personal experiences." When I pressed KH to consider sharing her experience in persisting and overcoming similar challenges to those her students were facing so as to become a successful professional, suddenly it made sense to her. She was talking about her successes but not her struggles. Students see us in our current position; they do not see or know the blood, sweat, and tears we shed on our pathway to achievement. When students meet us, they mistakenly see a finished product when in reality we are still on our journeys just as they are on theirs.

Next, I asked KH to think about her first experience when she was a nursing student and to share it with me. She shared her experience quite vulnerably. It was raw and real, to the extent that just talking about it was incredibly difficult for her and brought forth more emotion than either of us anticipated. But she worked through it.

Eventually, this experience led to the creation of her first Real Talk (see Appendix A). As we continued our work together, she also created alternative lessons (see Appendix A) and implemented them in her class. Her new Real Talk and alternative lessons led to an increase in students attending her support sessions and to improved student performance.

Encouraging students to voluntarily attend additional study times or school-related activities is challenging and often simply does not work. Accordingly, KH's success in increasing attendance at optional support sessions speaks volumes about her successful use of Real Talk. Student feedback provided further evidence. One student said, "You were definitely the most student success–oriented teacher I have ever had. I can directly link my success to the student support sessions you offered, and several fellow students agreed with me."

The evolution of KH's teaching was not a simple, one-step process. It took time, as do all things related to teaching and learning. Beyond committing her time, KH had to become comfortable with being vulnerable, and she had to learn how to be appropriately vulnerable with her students.

I want to be clear about this point of *appropriately* using vulnerability within Real Talk. Being vulnerable does not mean placing your burdens on your students' shoulders; they have enough to deal with already. In fact, "sharing yourself to teach or move a process forward can be healthy and effective, but disclosing information as a way to work through your personal stuff [and oversharing] is inappropriate and unethical" (Brown, 2015, p. 162). To underscore this point, I will share two examples of inappropriate Real Talks. Both instances involved people with whom I worked closely and who I know to have been wholeheartedly committed to increasing student success.

In the first example, the instructor inappropriately focused his Real Talks on his marriage problems. Talking about your marriage is not inherently inappropriate, but this teacher was venting about his personal struggles and unloading his emotional baggage on whoever would listen—in this case, his students. He thought his Real Talk went well because he felt better afterward, and the students listened to him quietly. But in reality, his students were uncomfortable with what he shared, and he provided no opportunity for them to engage with him before he moved on to teaching the curriculum.

I asked him to stop doing Real Talks until we could work together to make them more appropriate and properly structured. To his credit, he welcomed the feedback and continued refining his approach. It was a challenge for him, but through hard work, he developed appropriate and powerful Real Talks that transformed his relationship with students. He commented later, "Until I stepped back after we talked, I didn't realize what I was doing. I thought that by sharing intimate details about my life, I was connecting with my students. When it finally clicked for me, I was mortified by what I did. Now, I see the thoughtful, structured intentionality that goes into an appropriate Real Talk."

My second example is a teacher who engaged in inappropriate oversharing in her Real Talks. She too is highly committed to struggling students and intentionally seeks opportunities to interact with and teach student populations that some of her colleagues openly avoid. She was eager and ready to conduct a Real Talk, but she ended up sharing graphic details that were unnecessary and counterproductive. Thankfully, at that point she was just practicing with me and our colleagues!

This teacher's Real Talk described a medical procedure that had a deep and life-changing impact on her. Along the way, she gave vivid, detailed descriptions of what she went through in the hospital. Although medical procedures are a part of life, the graphic details she shared were not relevant to the point she was trying to make. Had it been a science or medical class, there might have been a rationale for disclosing these details, but she did not teach in those areas.

As we worked together, she refined and scaled back her sharing. She explained, "I care so much about my students, and I want them to know everything about me, just as I want to know everything about them. But I've come to realize that there are boundaries, and I need to make an intentional effort to stay within them." This teacher went on to create wonderful Real Talks and constructed life-changing experiences for many of her students.

Vulnerability is "based on mutuality and requires boundaries" (Brown, 2015, p. 45). A healthy and effective balance in this regard is best developed in an environment with colleagues who are also committed to the process of learning and applying Real Talk. Such a group can grow together by supporting and providing honest feedback to each other. Although you can certainly develop on your own, having access to helpful eyes, ears, hearts, and minds will give you quality feedback and insight that can accelerate your growth.

What does appropriate vulnerability look like in a Real Talk? That is a complicated but important question. There is no single way to be vulnerable within Real Talk. There is consistency in how genuine vulnerability is projected, but the content varies from person to person. One of the most common misconceptions is that Real Talk has to be profound, deeply emotional, or heart-wrenching. This is not true; vulnerability is not about unleashing the intimate self and a tidal wave of emotion. Instead, "vulnerability is the core of all emotions and feelings. To feel is to be vulnerable" (Brown, 2015, p. 33).

With this observation in mind, understand two things. First, the emotions and feelings within your Real Talk should stem from vulnerability; second, creating and sharing your Real Talk is courageous and inherently an act of vulnerability. I have heard effective Real Talks about a first pet, winning a sports event, overcoming a fear, feeling fortunate, and being a first-generation college student. To compare the subject of your Real Talk to someone else's is futile.

To further help you develop and apply vulnerability in your Real Talks, I have added new and varied examples to the appendix for you to explore. Keep in mind that as you embark on your journey with vulnerability by creating and refining your Real Talk, your story is no better or less valuable than another person's.

As you introduce vulnerability into the classroom through Real Talk, you set the stage for empathy. Once you connect with students, they will become comfortable with being vulnerable with you too. At this point, how you respond is paramount. I have too often seen missed opportunities for life-changing interactions between teachers and students due to a lack of empathy. This is understandable because learning to respond with empathy can also be a difficult process. Some people need to be taught how to express empathy, and others must search within themselves to decide if they are even willing to be empathetic. Many teachers believe that truth telling is powerful, especially in response to students' expressions of vulnerability. I agree, but how you tell the truth matters. Students need to know they are heard and understood, that they matter, and that you are trying to understand their situation. You must also be caring and compassionate. Without empathy, you won't be able to respond as students need you to respond.

Empathy

My preferred definition of "empathy" comes from Dr. Helen Riess (2018): "a human capacity consisting of several different facets that work together to enable us to be moved by the plight and emotions of others" (p. 10). Lack of empathy can have negative consequences in the classroom, especially when one is conducting Real Talks. As just noted, the point when a student is vulnerable with the teacher following a Real Talk is a crucial moment. Not knowing how to respond, the teacher may unintentionally act in an uncomfortable, indifferent, dismissive, or judgmental manner. This response harms the student–teacher relationship instead of strengthening the intended connection at which Real Talk aims.

Some teachers need guidance in expressing empathy when students open up to them as a result of Real Talk. Not knowing how to respond does not necessarily indicate an absence of empathy; it may just call for further effort concerning how to display empathy in the classroom. I do not want to give the impression that responding with empathy is easy. I initially struggled to respond with empathy to students. I have worked intentionally to develop empathy over the years, and I continue to work on it.

During my early years of teaching, anger stemming from my experiences with different forms of oppression blinded me and created a barrier between me and my students. There was a time when I mistakenly believed that because I had risen out of dire circumstances, anyone could do the same thing. I now know that life doesn't work that way. Previously, my focus was misdirected toward thinking that *I* had achieved everything *I* had accomplished. That was simply not true; I was only part of the formula for my success. You see, no one makes it alone: "not rock stars, not professional athletes, not software billionaires" (Gladwell, 2008, p. 115), not geniuses, and not me either! In fact, in my case a great number of people were instrumental in my success. Since I cannot acknowledge all of them here, I will settle for another story about my mentor.

When we first met, I was an undergraduate student who had just entered the university after completing community college. I was lost, nervous, and anxious, and I was experiencing daily reminders that I did not belong in college. When I showed up at his sociology class, I sat in the back corner, close to a window; being there gave me a vantage point from which to survey the entire room, as well as a rapid exit in case of an emergency. Every day, I waited to leave class last and would walk past the teacher as he shuffled around with his belongings.

One day, he surprised me as I was walking past. He leaned forward and said, "You know, it pushes me against the wall." I turned and, with an incredibly intense look on my face, retorted, "What did you say to me, old man?" He replied, "Oh, your hate. I can feel it, and it pushes me against the wall." I said, "What do you know about hate?" His response was brilliant: "I know it stems from pain. If you ever want to talk, I'm here." I walked away. Weeks passed before I decided to visit him during his office hours.

The teacher was focused on his work and startled when I walked in. I immediately said, "What do you know about pain?" He said he would be happy to talk about it, but not in his office. Instead, he gave me a day, time, and address and asked me to meet him there. I imagined that we would meet at a place of great significance or with powerful symbolism. I was wrong. He had given me the address for a chain restaurant.

When I showed up, he was already sitting at a table, drinking tea and eating a muffin. I joined him, and our life-changing conversation began. I shared my story with him, and he followed by sharing his. Toward the end of our conversation, he said with a laugh, "Look at us, two social deviants having breakfast." At that time in my life, I did not know how to smile outwardly, but I smiled and felt embraced on the inside. My mentor saw the whole person, not just my issues, struggles, or everything else that, at face value, seemed to make us complete opposites. His response to me was compassionate—"the warmhearted response to [someone's] suffering . . . [which is] the outward expression and evidence" of his empathy (Riess, 2018, p. 24). He approached me with empathy and compassion. This is the foundation of how you must respond to students once they share their vulnerability with you through Real Talk.

I have many examples of teachers responding with empathy to their students, but one in particular stands out. I worked with a chemistry teacher who had been incorporating Real Talk into his teaching for two years. He was elated with the connections he was making with his students. But he also shared an email regarding a student he thought he was not connecting with. This student was quiet and standoffish whenever the teacher tried to speak to her in class. In the middle of the semester, she sent him an email, thanking him for making the class interesting and helping her feel accepted. As the semester progressed, the two developed a good relationship. But this changed toward the end of the semester. The young woman did poorly on a few exams and was upset about it. She told the teacher she had studied and felt prepared but was disappointed with the outcome. The teacher listened, offered to review her exam to understand why she answered questions incorrectly, and suggested strategies to prepare for future exams. The student seemed receptive, but to the teacher's disappointment, the rest of the semester became difficult and painful.

Within a week of this conversation regarding the subpar exam, the student complained to the administration about an unfair grade. She initiated the complaint on her own and eventually involved her mother to further dispute the grade, contending that the student had been mistreated. The teacher was hurt, felt betrayed, and became angry over what he considered a false accusation.

As the semester progressed, the student did not relent regarding her grade complaint. I was impressed by how the teacher handled the situation. He listened to the student with curiosity and tried to understand rather than passing judgment—the essence of an empathetic response. Empathy does not encompass simply how you interpret or respond to someone else's feelings; it is a "delicate balance of appreciating the feelings of others and learning how to manage our own feelings so we can be helpful" (Riess, 2018, p. 12). Although he did not know the driving force behind the student's accusations, he was able to work through his own feelings and continue serving her as well as possible. He did not treat the student any differently than he had done before the accusation and continued trying to connect with her. In response, the student was never rude or disrespectful but became distant and cold toward the teacher. Eventually, the semester came to an end, with no change in the grade and no evidence that the teacher had acted unfairly.

The teacher tried to understand the student's perspective because he thought that something deeper and unseen was impelling the young woman to contest her grade. Ultimately, he was trying to understand the situation from the student's "physical, psychological, [emotional,] social, and spiritual perspective" (Riess, 2018, p. 23). He did not expect to ever find out what was really going on because this was the student's final semester before she graduated. But months later, he happened to encounter her and her mother in a local mall. To his surprise, the student apologized, assured the teacher that he had not done anything unfair, and thanked him for treating her so well even after the complaint. It turned out that the student had panicked over the test grade, fearing that a low final grade for the course could cause her to be denied acceptance to a university. The stakes were incredibly high for her because she was the first person in her family to attend college, so she lashed out at her teacher.

The teacher was fortunate to gain this insight from hearing the student's backstory. But the most important part of this episode is how the teacher remained consistently empathetic over time. This is crucial, especially when students are apathetic, combative, or disrespectful and you do not fully understand why.

I am not suggesting that teachers should become social workers, therapists, or counselors. Rather, I am advocating that we must not fail to learn from the voices of students. What we learn from students helps us connect them with the resources they need to overcome the barriers standing between them and success in school.

In one instance, a biology teacher brought a student to a school office that provided free clothes for students in need. The student needed clothes, but she was too embarrassed to visit the office independently. To help her become more comfortable with the situation and get the clothing she desperately needed, the teacher took the time to personally introduce her to the people in the office. Similarly, a history teacher who learned that a few students in her class needed food didn't just tell them about a local food pantry; she met them there after school and introduced them to the food pantry staff.

In another case, an English teacher learned two of her students were struggling to balance school with motherhood and work and needed help with child care. She connected the students to the appropriate person at school so they could get child care support. On their own, these students were either unaware of or unwilling to access the requisite support resources, but through their teachers, they could get what they needed.

Responding with empathy is not a matter of who is worthy. Students are worthy the moment they walk into your classroom. When we connect with them, we begin the process of acknowledging their worthiness. For some students, this may be the first time anyone has suggested they are worthy of a chance at success.

As we get to know our students' needs, we will find that they will vary widely. It is not our role to judge them but to embrace them and guide them with empathy. Empathy can take many forms, ranging from the examples I have provided to a caring look that shows students they matter. Students are works in progress—as we all are—and teachers play an important role in their journey. The students who struggle in our classes are not destined for failure or a desolate future. But their struggles are worsened when we treat them like inconveniences and judge them for the burdens they carry. We have the privilege of being in a position from which to respond with empathy and guide them, just as others have guided us to where we are today.

Growth Mindset

A growth mindset is best defined as "the belief that your basic qualities are things you can cultivate through your efforts, your strategies, and help from others. [Additionally,] everyone can change and grow through application and experience" (Dweck, 2017, p. 7). Growth mindset can be enhanced through a sense of purpose, a commitment to personal and professional development, and intentionality. I will focus specifically on how growth mindset relates to alternative lessons because you (the teacher) need a growth mindset to revisit and change how you deliver your curriculum to better serve students.

Developing a growth mindset is an incredibly difficult task, as it pushes us away from what is comfortable and familiar. I have met many teachers who knew their teaching practice was not effective but who confessed that they were uncomfortable, unmotivated, or scared by the thought of changing their approach or simply didn't know how to do it. For them, it was easier to stick with what they had always done, regardless of their students' outcomes. But if you want to grow, you must be willing to experiment and seek to improve, no matter how you think students or colleagues may judge you. In short, committing to a growth mindset is easier said than done.

One area where I struggled to grow was my willingness to become a mentor. I had benefited greatly from having a mentor, but even with that experience, I did not want to become one. The problem had nothing to do with the worthiness or potential of possible mentees; it all had to do with me. I viewed mentorship as challenging because I thought it would be extremely difficult to do for someone else what my mentor had done for me. I had no idea how he did it; I just knew how his guidance had changed the course of my life for the better. Thus, whenever I had the opportunity to be a mentor, I avoided it. At times, I summoned the courage to ease my way into being a mentor, but the moment I felt resistance or disagreement from a potential mentee, I quickly gave up. And I blamed the mentee instead of looking within myself to understand why I had quit and was unwilling to try.

In moments of greater clarity, I thought that perhaps I could be a good mentor, but my cynical side quickly jumped in, telling me it would be too hard to acquire the necessary skills and that trying would be useless. I also disregarded my colleagues who encouraged me to become a mentor and who provided advice on what I would have to learn to be a good one. Lastly, I was scared. I feared that I would be a bad mentor and ruin someone's life. I hid behind this fear and kept it to myself as I resisted becoming a mentor. My resistance was a classic illustration of a fixed mindset in action (Dweck, 2017).

Not until I met JH did I finally overcome my struggles to become a mentor. Stereotypically, I imagined that a mentor must be older than the mentee. JH showed me that this did not have to be the case; he was 16 years older than me. I was an adjunct instructor teaching an introductory sociology class at a community college, and he was in my class.

One day after class, JH stuck around to talk with me, and the conversation transitioned to why I was teaching and why he was in school. I learned that he had been a drug addict for 17 years and then clean for 10, but he felt as if he had accomplished nothing since getting off drugs, other than working odd jobs and avoiding ending up on the streets again. JH had returned to school with the hope of improving his people skills and eventually becoming a customer service representative for a large corporation. I casually suggested that he consider pursuing an associate degree, which could lead to more opportunities and higher pay. He replied, "Oh yeah, in what?" I told him he could get a degree in whatever he liked and get paid for doing something he enjoyed. He said, "Well, I like sociology; maybe I could get a degree in that." I urged him to consider other options because a sociology degree would require many more years of study, and it seemed that he wanted something sooner rather than later. As he walked out the door, he turned and said, "Well, maybe with your guidance, I can do something with sociology."

By the end of the semester, I knew JH well. On the last day of class, he came to me and said, "I made sociology my major. Will you help me with what to do? I mean, you did it, so you must know how others can do it too." I felt a wave of fear come over me. But instead of responding with negativity or anger, I overcame my fear and said humbly,

"I can try." He replied, "Thank you. People have never thought I was worth trying to help."

At that moment with JH, I embraced a growth mindset with regard to being a mentor. Trying to guide him led me beyond my classroom and into new areas within the realm of education. I started to grow as I learned about the services available in student affairs, different courses outside my own field, nearby schools and their transfer requirements, scholarships, and so much more that would benefit JH. Whenever I didn't have answers to JH's questions or didn't know how to guide him, I sought help from others.

Through my efforts to help JH, I also received help, and I grew as a mentor. I became better informed and developed new skills. I faced many obstacles and challenges as his mentor because he struggled to achieve what he had set out to do. There were also times when we disagreed or he resisted my guidance. Unlike before, I did not give up; instead, I searched for ways to overcome the situation. My confidence grew as I perceived my own abilities improving over the years.

Needless to say, JH grew too. From taking a few classes at the community college, he is now in the final stages of completing a doctoral degree. It was an incredible journey for both of us. I'm glad I pushed myself and kept assisting him even when I felt it would be easier to simply give up.

After I completed a presentation on professional development for teachers, a math teacher waited until everyone else had left and then approached me. She was struggling with how to help her lowest-performing students. "We have tried a variety of types of professional development to improve our students' success," she told me. "I have implemented what I learned. I also send emails to students who are not doing well. I am disappointed because I have made only a 3 percent increase in my students' success over three years, and now in my fourth year, I am stuck with no further increase. What more do I need to do to increase their success?"

First, I responded that a 3 percent increase over three years was a good start. I then asked her, "When you implemented the interventions, were you consistent, and did you work through the challenges of implementing them?" She answered, "No, I tried one, and when I didn't think it was working or it became complicated, I tried another. If things don't work right away, I get frustrated and just move on." I said to her, "If you want to work together, it is a three-year commitment, and you have to stick to what we do. If you can't do that, I suggest you not join the cohort." She paused for a bit and said, "Okay, thank you for letting me know." I figured that was the last I had seen of her.

To my surprise, she reached out to me later and said, "I will do it. But I want you to know I am going in as a skeptic. I will do everything you ask and stick with it, but I have my doubts." I responded, "Being a skeptic is fine. I just need you to fully commit to trying and sticking with it."

The math teacher did exactly what she said she would do. She followed everything I asked of her, even while commenting that she was unconvinced it would work. Slowly but surely, she changed from a skeptic to a believer. I remember as she shared the outcomes from her first Real Talk (on overcoming adversity) and alternative lesson. She was elated and couldn't believe what happened.

"When I finished," she explained to me, "I did not think it was effective. But after class, I had several students stay and eagerly share their struggles and successes with overcoming adversity. I have never had students stay after class and want to talk to me as much as they did, or especially talk about their struggles." She also had success with her alternative lessons. "With everything I am learning about my students, I created alternative lessons around their interests—starting their own business, the stock market, or career aspirations. I can connect math with all of it. Student engagement in class has increased dramatically," she said. The transformation she went through and, in turn, the transformation of her classes were remarkable. By the end of the academic year, her growth mindset served her well as we began to look at the data.

Every year, the schools I work with collect data to determine the effectiveness of the interventions related to our professional development. There is no expectation for teachers to collect their own data in addition to the institutional data. But this math teacher collected her own data and shared her findings. She had an 8 percent increase in students passing her class, a higher percentage of completed assignments, and an increase in students earning higher grades, along with more student engagement and interaction with her than ever before. Even outside the classroom, she was having positive experiences with students, which helped her discover the positive impact of her new approach in more detail.

Much of this teacher's success came from applying a growth mindset to her professional development. She did the work, kept with it, embraced her failures, and was open to constructive criticism and new learning. To be a great teacher, you must challenge yourself to keep learning new things and keep developing your ability to teach. I saw this math teacher embrace that philosophy, and her students benefited from her commitment.

No improvement of teaching can happen when a teacher has decided there is no room for improvement, that there is no time to improve, or that the students—not the teacher—are the problem. Whether you are using my approach or any other method, you must approach it with a growth mindset. Taking advantage of an opportunity for growth does not mean that you are currently an inadequate teacher. It means you understand that your development never ends, that you are committed to developing yourself further, and that you place your students first by your willingness to grow.

Creativity

When you teach, you must rid yourself of limiting thoughts and allow yourself to create freely. This mental freedom will propel you into a space primed for creativity. I view creativity in terms of three related ideas derived from the late Sir Ken Robinson, PhD: "*imagination*, which is bringing to mind things that are not present to our senses; *creativity*, which is the process of developing original ideas that have value; and *innovation*, which is the process of putting new ideas into practice" (S. K. Robinson, 2017, p. 2).

Students love to learn; I see proof of that every day. But students struggle to learn in classrooms that are not creative, engaging, and clearly relevant to their lives. We are deceiving ourselves if we think students are truly learning and developing skills while a teacher lectures at them or reads slides from a presentation. Few students learn in that manner, and teaching in that way is an injustice to those with other learning styles.

Teaching is not about how you learned when you were in school; instead, it is about how the students you are teaching today learn. The classroom should be a place where creativity is everywhere, not a place where it dies.

I urge teachers to fight complacency because it is the enemy of creativity. Implementing creativity into your teaching is hard work. You can't just pontificate about what should happen in the classroom; you have to keep coming up with new ideas.

My struggles with creativity have come and gone throughout my career. Having been told in school that I was not creative, I have frequently worried about what people would think of my ideas or doubted my innovative abilities. This struggle was often compounded by varying workplace norms and by pressure to increase student success. For example, when I proposed trying something new and creative in the classroom, I commonly received this reply: "That is not how we do things around here." If I actually implemented something creative, some of my colleagues would question whether my students were actually learning—because they were having "too much fun." When my creativity in the classroom incorporated relevance, engagement, inclusiveness, and increased student success, some colleagues accused me of "dumbing down" the curriculum. Within specialized programs, administrators were terrified of not meeting student success goals, so anything that deviated from what they considered the best approach was frowned upon. I would be "talked to" so that I would "get with the program."

In my experience, the intense focus on meeting short-term benchmarks was the main factor keeping administrators and colleagues from seeing how other teaching methods could be even more effective in helping students succeed. But to be fair, sometimes my creativity was inhibited by self-imposed behaviors. On occasion, I developed an alternative lesson and then convinced myself the idea was not creative and shelved it. In other cases, if an innovative approach did not go as well as I had hoped, I interpreted the result as proof that I was not creative. At still other times, I found myself avoiding creativity altogether. I did not want to stick out or be singled out, and it seemed easier to conform. I also felt alone because I had no community of thought partners pushing me to be more creative, which would have made a positive difference for me. These struggles are far from unique to me. I have heard from thousands of educators who reported having similar experiences or worse in their own careers.

Although I have come a long way, I still find deploying creativity challenging at times. This is normal. But I have come to appreciate that the creative process often leads to innovation through "a series of repetitive failures" (Ashton, 2015, p. 63). In other words, creativity typically does not just happen. Instead, it emerges from your imagination and evolves through many steps as you observe, evaluate, go through iterations, and attempt to solve challenges that lead to being creative (Ashton, 2015). Creativity is ongoing, cyclical, and experimental. This realization helped me push myself to continue developing my creativity, despite my preconceived notion that I was not the creative type. Additionally, the incredible teachers I have worked with have served as inspirations.

DJ, a biology teacher, sets a great example of embracing and implementing creativity in his classroom through Real Talk and alternative lessons. He challenges the misconception that creativity is more easily applied in the arts, humanities, and social sciences than in the physical sciences. I met DJ when he participated in a professional development program I delivered at his school. He is a white man teaching in a school where 54 percent of students are racial minorities and 66 percent are in remedial classes. I was immediately impressed by his enthusiasm, humility, and willingness to try new things in the classroom.

We began our work during the summer, with 15 teachers from various subject areas, as part of a first-year professional development cohort in a three-year program. The teachers spent four intensive days with me, six hours each day. During our time together, they learned, created, practiced, and implemented Real Talks and alternative lessons, which they presented to their colleagues and me as if we were students in their classroom. It was an outstanding group of teachers, but even among the superb talent in the first cohort, DJ stood out. His Real Talks and alternative lessons reflected a clear understanding that subject matter expertise is not enough to make someone a great teacher. DJ wanted to improve as a better teacher, and he approached this training as an opportunity to create an environment where his students would be eager to learn. His growth was enhanced and accelerated by the professional development environment in which the cohort members supported one another in improving and refining their creativity.

Over our first two years together, I saw DJ have an incredible impact through making Real Talk and alternative lessons his own. His Real Talks intentionally addressed specific struggles his students were dealing with or might face both within and outside school. Some examples of his topics included managing and balancing personal life and school, facing struggles, addressing student fatigue, enjoying success, and using failure to reignite a love for learning.

Although DJ's Real Talks (see Appendix B) were unique and effective and his creative delivery was a work of art, here I will focus on his alternative lessons, which marked a major shift from his traditional style—namely, lectures accompanied by notes projected on a screen. In his alternative lessons, he embedded a question-based learning format to increase students' understanding and long-term retention of concepts. The alternative lessons guided students through the material while increasing their engagement and focus. He designed each one as part of a layered structure, relating each new concept to prior concepts, which helped to incorporate repetition into student learning and solidify their understanding of the material presented (see Appendix B).

To assess the effectiveness of his alternative lessons relative to his traditional lectures, DJ randomly selected different individual units from his curriculum in which he used either format. He measured his students' feelings of connection with him and their understanding of the class material by administering anonymous online surveys throughout the semester to evaluate the students' enjoyment of the course material. Furthermore, he used examination grades to determine whether any difference existed in students' understanding of concepts between alternative and traditional lessons. He then analyzed the data through a mixed-methods design using data analytics software. Figures 3.1, 3.2, 3.3, and 3.4 illustrate what he found.

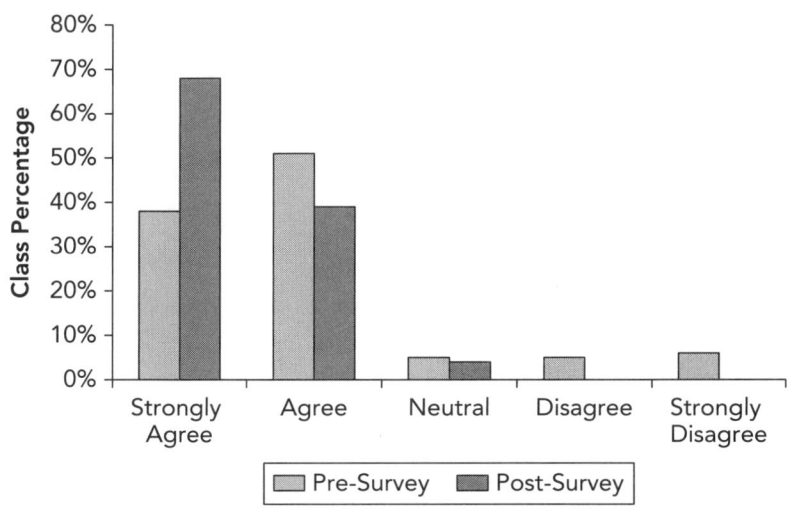

Figure 3.1 Students' Satisfaction With Ability to Make Connection With Instructor (Increased From 89.7% to 97.1%)

Figure 3.2 Student Comfort With Course Materials (Increased From 82.8% to 97.1%)

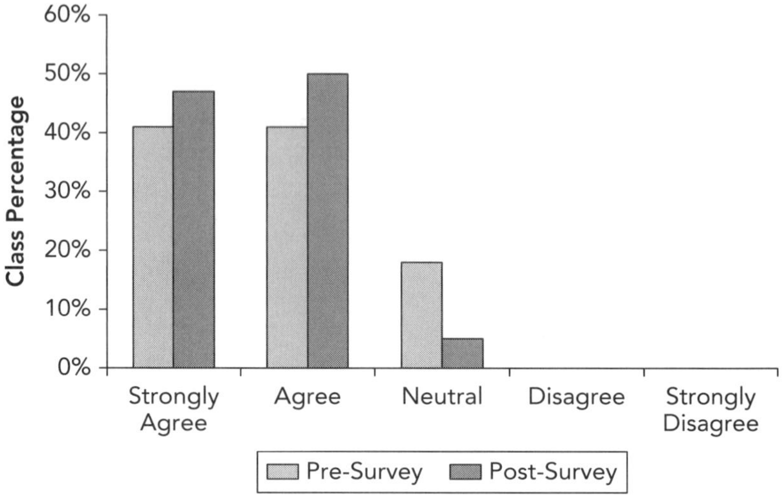

Pre-Survey / Post-Survey

Figure 3.3 Enjoyment of Material (61% vs. 76.5%)

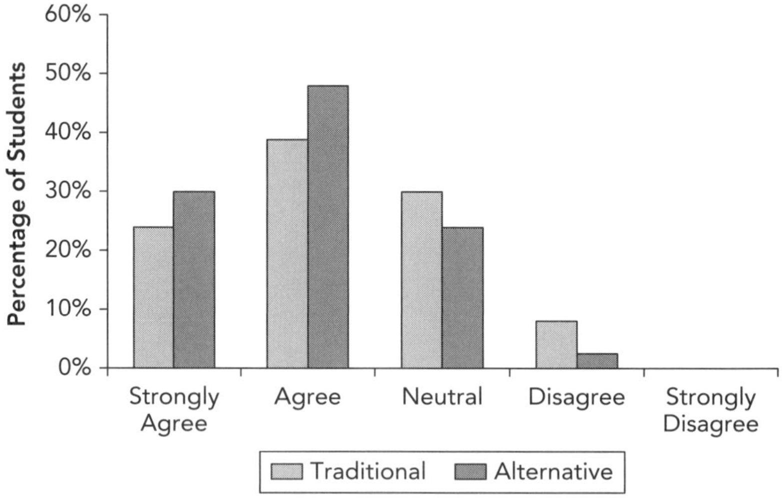

Traditional / Alternative

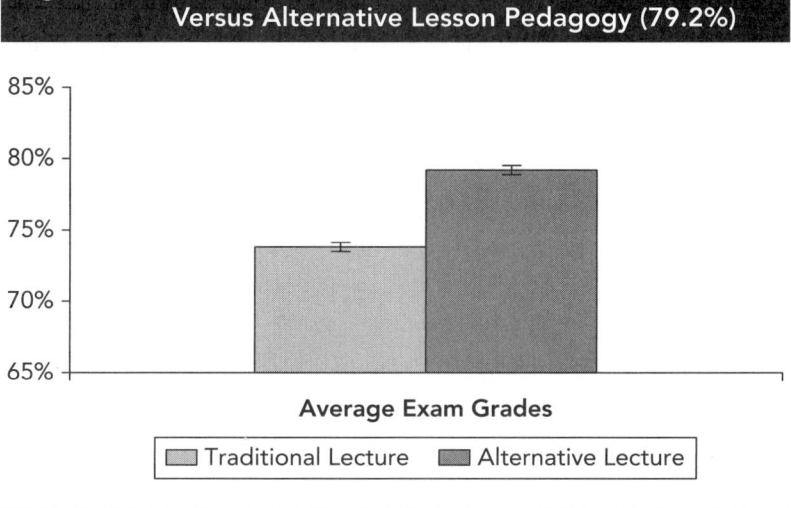

Figure 3.4 Exam Scores: Traditional Lectures (73.8%) Versus Alternative Lesson Pedagogy (79.2%)

The difference was significant at $p = 0.023$.

DJ's findings indicated that his new approach was more effective than his traditional approach had been and that it had a direct positive impact on students' grades. Through the creativity of his alternative lessons, he engaged students' curiosity and brought out the best in them. He put his imagination to work by incorporating his students' interests and life experiences into his classroom, and the effort paid off by increasing their success.

DJ could have just stuck with his old ways and made no changes in his teaching. Instead, he confronted what he viewed as a problem—low student success rates—and took steps to solve it. He didn't treat his students as the problem. Nor did he simply talk in meetings about his passion for biology and his commitment to student success. Instead, he took action by getting involved in professional development to improve his classroom teaching and better serve his students. He did the necessary work to apply his creativity in the classroom. There were no shortcuts—even he had his good and bad days—but through that process, he developed into an excellent teacher.

In my conversations with DJ, I found him to be continually reflecting on his progress, learning deeply and getting to know his classroom technique better. I continue to work with him and admire how he has developed his unique approach grounded in PRT. More importantly, he has continued to increase student success. Combining his passion with knowledge, structure, and strategy has resulted in a consistently creative classroom environment.

All people have their own approach to creativity, but regardless of one's approach, hard work is unavoidable. Teachers, like DJ, with the courage to apply their creativity in the classroom persevere through self-doubt, contempt from colleagues or students, and failure until they create something unique and effective. Without creativity in the classroom, we damage students' inclination to learn and limit the learning environment.

Everyone can be creative, and you don't need permission or affirmation to try. Give your heart, mind, and soul the freedom to be the best version of your creative self. Through Real Talk and alternative lessons, you can bring your creativity to life in the classroom, and students will directly benefit from it.

GRIT

Dr. Angela Duckworth (2018), a recognized expert on the concept of grit, says that it requires passion, perseverance, strategy, and continued development of knowledge so as to achieve one's goals. In the context of PRT, grit is the fifth component teachers can leverage to evolve teaching in the classroom—as opposed to what we tell students *they* need in order to be successful.

I want to be clear from the start about what grit does *not* do. Grit does not remove the institutional barriers within our society that teachers and students face daily. In school settings, those barriers include inequities in school funding and teacher pay. Within a larger context, racial, social, gender, sexual orientation, and economic injustice continuously oppress students and teachers. No amount of grit can magically make these barriers go away.

For me, grit is present in my earliest memories, as my mother prepared me for a world in which people would hate or be scared of me without even knowing me and would block my attempts to succeed. I have also applied grit throughout my professional career when dealing with unnecessary obstacles from the types of people my momma equipped me to encounter. The fact that I achieved personal and professional success partly through grit does not guarantee that anyone else will overcome the disadvantages unfairly imposed on them. Overcoming oppression and adversity is a far more complicated matter that would require another book to unpack.

So what can we do with grit, as teachers? I urge teachers, as part of their commitment to justice, to apply their grit to increasing the success of their neediest students. This application is not easy. It requires intentionality in how and when we apply it in PRT and is further enhanced through earnest guidance from others.

As a model for your development of grit, I will discuss how I used it to improve my teaching and student success in an alternative education program. I was part of a small but mighty team of colleagues who were wholeheartedly committed to our students' success. Like the other teachers, I wore many hats and did far more than teaching. We took turns carrying an emergency phone so that someone would be available 24 hours a day, seven days a week in case of a student emergency. In alternative education, those emergencies can include students being arrested or kicked out of their homes, drug overdoses, instances of abuse, severe hunger, or other life circumstances out of their control. We also frequently helped students with their medical needs and connected them to doctors, as well as enabled them to obtain government-issued identification cards and driver's licenses.

On other occasions, students would stop attending classes and we would have to go looking for them to make sure they were alive and safe. Once we found them, we would seek to help them come back to school and finish what they had set out to do. Students would sometimes lash out and become disrespectful or belligerent toward teachers and administrators. There were new challenges every day.

It would have been easier to walk away from this very tough environment instead of staying to support my students. I especially found it challenging because I too had experienced much of what they were going through. On my worst days, I took things personally because I felt their disrespect was intentional. But through self-reflection in moments of frustration, I combined my passion with perseverance. I felt passionate about my students' success and reminded myself that they needed to be supported with empathy and compassion to address their struggles, just as others had done for me. Instead of taking things personally, I knew I had to persevere as their teacher because they needed a commitment from me.

I also had to become strategic in how I supported my students and more thoughtful in approaching each of them and their unique needs and struggles. There was no blanket solution for each obstacle we encountered. As I learned from my students, I developed knowledge and insight regarding how best to serve them. I also learned from my colleagues, and we shared information about resources or personal insights about our students with each other. It is easy to give up on students and much harder to remain their most committed advocate. I stayed loyal to my students because I was deeply committed to them, and I believe my grit contributed greatly to their success.

I first met CH at a student success conference where I was a keynote speaker. She attended my follow-up session, and I was immediately struck by her passionate commitment to improving her approach in the classroom. This connection was the beginning of many years of working together as she learned PRT and applied it in her classroom. Through CH, I learned that half of her school's students who had been placed on academic probation were being dismissed for not meeting their academic requirements. She strongly believed that her school had an ethical responsibility to support these students as much as possible to help them succeed. As a result, she created and taught in a holistic student success and engagement program aimed at students who were on academic probation or who had been dismissed from school but then readmitted through this program.

CH taught the mandatory academic recovery course, within which she implemented both Real Talk (see Appendix C) and alternative lessons. Although CH was committed to serving her students, she doubted herself and feared that she would fail. Her academic recovery courses were disproportionately composed of students of color, relative to the demographic composition of the predominately white school.

CH, who is white, openly shared her concerns with me. She felt a barrier between herself and her students based on their differences in age, socioeconomic background, experiences, and especially race. She feared not being able to connect with her students—particularly that her race would be an obstacle in earning their trust and teaching them effectively. She worried that her students' lived experiences with racial injustice and mistreatment would undermine her best efforts.

CH had to overcome her hesitation and fear, but thankfully, she had passion and purpose, along with "the intention to contribute to the well-being of others" (Duckworth, 2018, p. 143). Still, she needed guidance, support, and development to tap into her grit and fully commit herself despite her fears. CH identified her fears as additional challenges to overcome rather than allowing them to derail her, and she began working with her students in new ways.

I watched CH apply her grit on her journey to implementing Real Talk and alternative lessons. Through her grit, her thoughtful self-reflection, and her new pedagogical approach, she embraced the importance of touching the hearts and spirits of her students of color as part of the teaching and learning process. Without grit, she would not have made it through the intensive process she imposed upon herself. She learned and further developed her approach as she embraced a two-way relationship with her students, affirming the concept of student as teacher and teacher as student. In learning from them and the experiences they shared, CH became better informed of how to effectively teach them.

As CH successfully connected with her students, their classroom performance improved, but this upturn did not remove the obstacles they continued to face outside the classroom. Her students sought second and third chances to continue their education, but for a plethora of reasons, their actions did not always align with their desires. Through her connections with them, CH became uniquely aware of their struggles and relentlessly supported them.

Two memorable examples exhibit CH's commitment to her students. A young Mexican American male student from a poverty-stricken background—the first person in his family to be born in America—grew up accustomed to hard work, picking blueberries. He was dismissed from school and readmitted through her program. When he came back, he formed a strong connection with CH in class. Not only did he successfully pass her class, but he came back and attended it again the next semester without officially enrolling! Throughout his schooling, various legal issues had dragged him into court, and financial struggles and family problems also functioned as barriers to his success. As he continued to grow, CH eventually gave him opportunities to mentor other students and to take on various leadership roles within her program. She also supported him as he created an award-winning student organization that championed issues of social justice.

In another example, an African American male—also dismissed and then readmitted through her program—formed a powerful relationship with CH in her classroom and continued working with her even after passing the class. As he progressed in school, he faced many challenges: housing insecurity, financial struggles, difficulties in other teachers' classes, and a need to learn how to advocate for himself. CH not only supported him through these issues but also opened up opportunities for him to advance his leadership skills within her program. He became a mentor to other students, sharing his Real Talk with them and stepping into leadership positions throughout the school.

Both of these students were committed to succeeding in school, but outside forces beyond their control and poor decisions had jeopardized their success. Of course, poor decision-making can hamper the entire spectrum of students, but students of color suffer more severe judgments and penalties for their misguided actions (Mediratta et al., 2016). CH worked to understand the root causes underlying her students' poor decisions and helped them reconceptualize the pathways to their future. Helping them develop self-awareness, reframe the reasons for their failures, change their thinking about themselves and their choices, and increase their own belief in their worth and abilities was pivotal.

CH could have discontinued her support of these young men; instead, she persisted at their side. She proved that along with her enthusiasm about working with students, she had an endurance fueled by her grit. Her students taught her through their stories and experiences that the environment in which people grow up matters. This knowledge further inspired her commitment as she learned about the injustices her students had experienced. The fear she held when I first met her was transformed into an unwavering commitment to her students. She experienced their grit, and it inspired her own.

CH decided to become a resource for students trying to overcome the obstacles that pervaded their school and life experiences. She committed herself to equity by serving her students both inside and outside the classroom. Note that equity does not simply mean equality. CH's students needed extra investment due to their circumstances, and she recognized the importance of supporting students differently based on their individual needs. Pedagogically, she was willing to try something new in her classroom. Collectively, her hard work and that of her students paid off in the program's success rate, with an 80 percent retention rate over two years. In addition to increasing student retention, CH noted that her students demonstrated improved study skills and increased their study time.

Overall, CH's grit was impressive as she dedicated herself to helping her students graduate from school, attain successful careers, and live fulfilled lives. CH's strategies were so successful that her program won awards within her school and from an outside entity. Again, we cannot promise that these results will happen everywhere because grit alone does not lead to higher rates of student success, but it is one important contributing factor, especially within the context of Real Talk and alternative lessons.

Grit plays an important role in further developing your teaching and maintaining your commitment to students. Both of those tasks are incredibly taxing. However, if you dedicate yourself to developing and implementing grit on your journey to become a better teacher, the payoff will be priceless. You will see your classroom become an environment where students learn, develop, and begin to take steps toward achieving their dreams. When this type of classroom exists, we see what Nietzsche observed: "With everything perfect, we do not ask how it came to be. We rejoice in the present fact as though it came from out of the ground by magic" (cited in Duckworth, 2018, p. 39).

Creating a successful learning environment and improving your teaching do not happen by magic; they take time, effort, and definitely grit. Every successful teacher I have encountered has been tested throughout her or his career. Grit will serve you well as it served them—along with vulnerability, empathy, growth mindset, and creativity—to help you grow into a great teacher through Real Talk and alternative lessons.

Combining Forces

Although each concept discussed in this chapter can stand alone, they are most powerful when intentionally combined and are all necessary to implement PRT effectively. The examples and descriptions provided can help you navigate the intricacies often taken for granted or dismissed when people are attempting Real Talk and alternative lessons. To do this work, you must start by looking inward and being honest about your willingness to adopt what I have shared and make it true about yourself. Take time to reflect deeply on your teaching, and you will notice that you are getting to know yourself better too.

I am not asking you to abandon your existing style of teaching. Rather, I am asking you to absorb a new approach and build on what you are already doing so as to achieve higher success levels with students. The strategy of pairing Real Talk and alternative lessons in the classroom draws on all five behaviors discussed in this chapter—vulnerability, empathy, growth mindset, creativity, and grit—to open the door to authentic connections with students and construct a relevant, engaging, and inclusive curriculum in your classroom. In turn, this environment creates a space where students feel safe enough to be vulnerable, respond to and develop empathy, adopt their own growth mindset, tap into and explore their creativity, and recognize and foster grit.

To teach is to love to learn, and the more you learn as a teacher, the more students will benefit from what you have to teach them. Benjamin Franklin said, "There are three sorts of people in the world: those who are immovable, those who are movable, and those who move" (cited in Robinson & Aronica, 2015, p. 251). *Immovable* teachers don't want to change and see no reason to change their classroom teaching, even if the data suggest otherwise. *Movable* teachers are amenable to change; they recognize the need for change but need help learning what and how to change. Lastly, teachers who *move* are visionaries who implement new classroom strategies and envision a future different from their current reality. They are trailblazers committed, whether with or without the support of others, to transforming teaching and learning so as to achieve new and higher levels of success for their students.

As in all things, change is coming for better or worse, and schools and teachers cannot avoid this reality. I am hoping for better, and through my work, I try to contribute to that direction. Will you be left behind and replaced because of your unwillingness to move? Or will you take action to help mold and reshape the future of teaching and learning?

4

The Opportunity Gap, Demographic Shift, PRT, and a Sense of Belonging

The persistent gap in achievement between white and underrepresented students in the United States is universally acknowledged and has been the focus of extensive research. I began studying this issue more than 12 years ago, comparing white students to African American and Latinx students. Additionally, the achievement gap includes comparisons "between students in poverty and wealthier students, between [students with] parents [who have] little formal education and with greater formal education, and between English learners and native English speakers" (Carter & Welner, 2013, p. 2). I concluded, like most researchers (especially in sociology), that powerful factors beyond the classroom have contributed to creating and sustaining the achievement gap. Specifically, I argued for a "spectrum approach" to identifying ways to reduce and ultimately eliminate the achievement gap.

Over time, scholars, researchers, and practitioners have begun referring to the "opportunity gap" rather than an achievement gap. This terminology "shifts our attention from outcomes to inputs—to the deficiencies in the foundational component of societies, schools, and communities that produce significant differences in educational—and ultimately socioeconomic—outcomes" (Carter & Welner, 2013, p. 3). The opportunity gap highlights ways in which unequal opportunities cause the achievement gap within schools. In contrast, a narrow perspective focusing strictly on the achievement gap can give the impression that students are the problem rather than acknowledging the educational and societal factors influencing students' success in school.

I remember a student who would get up in the morning, go to a local gas station near his home, and ask for spare change. He was trying to collect enough money to ride the bus to and from school. Another student saw her family fractured by eviction from their apartment, as the family members had to split up and move in with different people. The student lived with friends, distant relatives, and anywhere else she could find shelter and food. She also worked part-time but did not earn enough money to survive on her own. Moreover, both of these students were racial minorities. Obviously, their daily struggle to survive impacted their ability to succeed in school. "Learning and life chances depend on key out-of-school factors such as health, housing, nutrition, safety, and enriching experiences, in addition to opportunities provided through formal elementary and secondary school preparation" (Carter & Welner, 2013, pp. 2–3). Therefore, it is crucial to acknowledge and account for the external factors that affect students' success.

In addition to a widening opportunity gap, we are experiencing a demographic shift within education. Racial diversity in schools has been increasing and will continue to do so. From fall 2000 to fall 2017, the percentage of white students in public elementary and secondary schools has decreased (National Center for Education Statistics [NCES], 2020). Schools (including community colleges and universities) not currently experiencing this change will eventually see it reach their own student population; whether it happens at a particular school in five years or 20 years, it is only a matter of time. Increased immigration and higher birth rates among people of color than among whites will add to increased racial diversity. These trends are not new or surprising. But they indicate that if our education system performs poorly in supporting students of color and those from lower socioeconomic backgrounds, as it has been doing consistently for decades, the social consequences will be enormous.

I have experienced the impact of this demographic shift in different ways—at one school where it occurred slowly over time and in another institution where a notable demographic change happened within a few years. In both cases, most teachers were white and the student body had historically been predominantly white. The teachers and students were present within the same school environment, but their experiences and perspectives were very different. Unfortunately—and unnecessarily—these differences led to conflict. Some teachers became disciplinarians trying to keep things as they "used to be" within their schools. Such a desire to maintain how things "used to be," in the context of a demographic shift, is dangerous and potentially explosive, as it can readily be perceived as a veiled form of racism, classism, or nativism. Meanwhile, other teachers responded to the changes at these schools by retiring or resigning. Among the teachers who stayed, most were committed to serving their new student population, but they struggled to teach students of color successfully, causing overall school outcomes to slip.

These remaining, committed teachers had several essential traits in common, including an equity-minded perspective, which is, according to McNair and colleagues (2020),

> a mode of thinking exhibited by practitioners who are willing to assess their own racialized assumptions, to acknowledge their lack of knowledge in the history of race and racism, to take responsibility for the success of historically underserved and minoritized student groups, and to critically assess racialization in their own practices as educators. (p. 20)

These teachers did not blame students for struggling to learn. Instead, they acknowledged that their own perspectives could be clouded by what they did not know or understand about their students, and they sought to learn from their students. Additionally, they believed that their students needed to know they mattered to the teachers and that students needed to see this authentically from teachers. Within a particular historical context and through their personal experiences, students frequently receive messages that they are less valuable than others, not good enough, and not worthy of success. The teachers rejected the underlying contemporary and historical dogmas that have perpetuated racial injustice and, instead, opened themselves up to learning new things that could add to or replace past practices. Additionally, they acknowledged the opportunity gap and embraced further development as necessary to become excellent teachers and reduce the opportunity gap.

Whenever we discuss the opportunity gap, especially in settings experiencing demographic shifts, it's important to acknowledge that certain things are beyond teachers' control. Systemic societal issues impacting students outside the classroom cannot be resolved in the classroom. However, teachers who choose to develop and deliver excellent teaching are more likely to positively impact student performance and thereby reduce the opportunity gap. In studies of the opportunity gap, good teaching has been identified as a primary variable. "The cumulative differences in access to key educational resources that support learning . . . at school [include] expert teachers, personalized attention, high-quality curriculum opportunities, good educational materials, and plentiful information resources" (Carter & Welner, 2013, p. 77). Schools that view teachers as an essential and valuable resource for student success are more likely to invest in developing expert teachers. Additionally, teachers must commit themselves to constant improvement in the classroom by using professional development opportunities available both within their school and elsewhere. Learning new pedagogical approaches such as PRT helps teachers increase student success overall, particularly with students of color or from lower socioeconomic backgrounds.

The power of PRT has been observed in case studies across the educational spectrum, where it positively affected teachers and, most importantly, students. The next two case studies, both involving students of color, illustrate the impact of PRT in classroom settings.

The first case study focuses on DL, an African American male who was attending an inner-city high school with a predominantly African American population. I worked with DL as part of an innovative class the school created with a nonprofit organization. The purpose of the class was to help students identify and share their dreams and then to help them take realistic steps to achieve those dreams. I was a frequent guest speaker in the class and became a mentor for some students.

I met DL in a class setting where I introduced myself through Real Talk. Some students were paying attention to every word I said, a few had their heads down, and a handful continued to talk as I spoke. DL was one of the students listening with rapt attention. After the class, he and a few other male students approached me to say how impressed they were by my message and what I shared about myself. DL specifically said, "You touched my soul, Dr. Paul. The struggle is real, and you didn't try to hide it like other teachers do. You made me feel hope, motivated, and that I matter because you shared your story with us." I was floored by his response and thanked him for his encouraging words. Eventually, I began to mentor DL, and we met one-on-one whenever I could make the time available when visiting his school. Through his class and our mentoring sessions, I used Real Talk, which led to an incredible experience for both of us.

Real Talk provided DL with a personalized educational experience, showing him that he mattered and connecting him with an educator within his school environment. It also gave DL a space where he felt safe to share his experience as a young African American man. For example, I learned that DL was the oldest of eight siblings. He felt fortunate to have two parents, but both worked incredibly long hours to provide for the family. DL's parents also helped other family members by allowing them to move into the home or by supporting them financially. DL's parents worked so much that he felt responsible for ensuring that his siblings were doing okay while his parents were at work. DL felt he had no one to consult for consistent, positive advice on how to achieve his goals.

DL shared another common problem: Drugs and violence were encouraged and respected in his neighborhood. In his world, many kids thought you weren't anyone unless you were a gang member or selling drugs. DL admitted that he had fallen into this trap by hanging out with drug dealers and students who seldom attended class, thinking it would bring him popularity and love from his peers. Instead, it got him arrested right in front of his school. He shared a vivid description of the shame he saw on his mother's face as she watched him placed into a police car, and he recalled the process of being fingerprinted and thrown into a jail cell as if he was just another criminal. DL realized that jail was a place where his dreams would die.

I met DL at a crucial point in his life, at a time when he wanted to make changes but did not know how to do so and felt inadequately supported and misunderstood by his school. He was ready to drop out of high school and transition from his part-time job as a warehouse custodian to full-time work.

During one of our mentoring sessions, DL shared that our conversations helped him feel good about himself. He also indicated his intention to leave school and go to work full-time instead of attending college because he thought he did not belong in school. I could see that he wanted to give up on himself. This conversation with DL led to a pivotal Real Talk based on unique moments in our relationship, "You Belong" (see Appendix D). This Real Talk impacted both DL and me profoundly. Even in our limited time together, we had a powerful and positive impact on each other's lives. One does not need countless hours, months, or years together to have a transformative experience; it can also happen in a few minutes within an individual conversation. In this case, Real Talk opened the door for a transformative experience between DL and me. I was intentional with my unconditional support, learning about DL's experiences and making sure he knew he mattered.

What this meant to DL is best described in his own words. They have been preserved because several colleagues surprised me with a video of DL, captured for a documentary about the students we were working with. In a short clip, DL spoke about what our relationship had meant to him, saying, "I want to be how Dr. Paul is to us." My colleague asked him, "How is [Dr. Paul] to you?" DL answered,

> He is someone we look forward to being around. He is down to earth, he is real. . . . I just love being in his presence. . . . I know that as soon as I walk up to him and give him the five, he is going to be nothing but real. . . . He asks me, "How are you doing? What are you working on? And how can I help?" . . . He has so much stuff going on, and he still acknowledges what I am doing, and he is still willing to take time out of everything he does. . . . He's still willing to be like, "Anytime you need me, I'm gonna be there—just let me know."

DL's perception of me and my value to him had nothing to do with my degrees, awards, or professional position. Most important to DL were the actions I took to show him that he matters and that I genuinely cared about him, all of which I could best convey through Real Talk. DL was surprised that I took an interest in him because he was accustomed to teachers and administrators looking for ways to control him rather than understand him. As DL gained confidence, his willingness to reengage in school increased, and he decided to make some of his dreams a reality.

DL dreamed of making a positive impact in his school. Through the class to which I referred earlier, he received the support, structure, and environment he needed to create a student–teacher dialogue and a "fly day Friday." DL felt there was a toxic environment between teachers and students in his school, and he wanted to change that. With my guidance and support, DL approached the administration and teachers to discuss his ideas and how he planned to facilitate the student–teacher dialogue. I provided some direction, but DL did the work, and it paid off as the administration and teachers supported his idea. I was not there when the dialogues took place, but through colleagues and DL, I learned that they were successful in easing tensions within the school and creating a platform for student voices to be heard and understood.

DL's proposal for a "fly day Friday" involved having seniors dress professionally on Fridays as an indication that they felt positive and hopeful about themselves and their futures. He understood that one of the biggest obstacles to this proposal was that, like himself, many of his peers could not afford professional attire. We brainstormed possible options, and DL decided to seek clothing donations from corporations. On his own accord, DL went to the downtown business district in his city and attempted to speak with executive-level professionals at major companies. Again, his hard work paid off, and he successfully secured the needed clothing donations.

Subsequently, when I visited DL's school on a Friday, I was greeted by him and other seniors dressed in suits and similar professional attire. It was beautiful to see his ideas come to fruition and even more exciting to see a young man, previously pegged as an almost-certain dropout, become engaged and experience success in endeavors that even most professionals would struggle with.

As the months progressed, our time together slowly diminished, and ultimately, we lost contact. But then our paths crossed again. I traveled to a university to deliver a series of workshops and then a keynote speech. Following an incredibly long day of presentations, I was escorted to the keynote location, exhausted and trying not to collapse while preparing mentally for the 200 to 400 people the university expected to attend (and while also attempting to manage my own turnout expectations of around 100). When we reached the auditorium, I was shocked to see almost 1,000 people there. Even more shocking, one of them was DL. As I walked to my seat in the front of the room, there he was, smiling from ear to ear. We instantly hugged each other and I said to him, "I told you that you would make it. This is just the beginning for you, and I am so proud of you!"

DL and I both choked up as he shared with me what he was doing at the university. DL was elated to be there, especially after nearly deciding to skip college and feeling as if he did not belong in school. He had done the hard work and earned his way into a university despite all his life challenges. The teachers who touched DL's heart and spirit were a vital part of his education process. The main thing he needed was teachers who would attempt to understand him instead of prejudging and punishing him. Without them, my supportive role in his journey probably would have had limited lasting impact.

My second case study, MH, is also an African American male who grew up in poverty in a large city. He enrolled in one of my sociology classes at a community college. He was quiet, focused, and trying to find his place at college. Early in the semester, through a Real Talk I conducted in my class, I struck a chord with MH. MH stayed after class and had many questions about my life. I answered his questions, and he shared stories about his own life with me. We spoke for over an hour.

After that, it became routine for him to stay after class and talk with me. I learned that when MH was in high school, he was an excellent student, with plans to go on to a university. No one in MH's family had attended college, and he was proud to be on a college trajectory. But in MH's final semester of high school, his best friend, who was like a brother to him, was murdered. Devastated by the tragedy, MH completely disengaged from his school, which provided no support and allowed him to disengage rather than investigating the sudden change in his behavior and school performance.

MH graduated from high school but did not go on to college. Instead, he turned to a life of crime for several years. Following an arrest and facing years in prison, MH decided to change his life. Fortunately, he avoided prison, discontinued his illegal activities, and began working at minimum-wage service jobs. MH knew that to improve his life situation, he would have to return to school. But he struggled in college, not due to lack of ability but because of the disconnect between him and his teachers and their teaching methods.

MH began to reconnect with school when he was exposed to Real Talk, which inspired the necessary student–teacher connection, and then to alternative lessons that reengaged him in classroom learning. MH said that he could relate to the lessons and examples I used to teach the subject matter in my class, even when something initially seemed far removed from his own experience. He said he needed this experience and that it was distinctly different from his other classes, where he felt his background, perspective, and culture were not incorporated in the teachers' lessons. MH believed that his other teachers lacked familiarity with his background and culture and had no interest in learning more about him. In those classrooms, the material was taught as if all students were the same and learned in the same way. As a result, he felt it was unsafe to engage intellectually. Unnecessarily and tragically, this cultural disconnect was hindering the development of MH's bright and curious mind.

Conversely, in my class MH was fully engaged, and we developed a positive relationship. As his trust in me grew, he confided in me that, although he wanted to continue with his education, he was afraid. When I asked MH what he was afraid of, his answer was a familiar one: "I am scared that being Black is going to affect me negatively in school." I could see the worry and pain on his face, and his words had the same impact on me. MH went on to share how much he appreciated that I could "feel" his struggle.

We remained in contact beyond that semester, and I had the privilege of being a positive force for him through his educational experience. As MH continued his educational journey, personal challenges continued to threaten his ability to succeed in school. He was attending school full-time and working full-time at a low-paying job. He lived in fear of the devastating impact that just one unexpected expense could have on his life trajectory. Eventually, this fear was realized when his car required repairs that he could not afford.

MH's first instinct was to reach out to his teachers and speak to them about his situation, to see if they would be flexible with him as he tried to find a solution to his problem. Unfortunately, he received responses like "It's not my problem," "You need to just work harder," and "School needs to be your priority." Unfortunately, these types of responses were the norm in MH's experience. Such disconnected and cold responses have no place in any educational setting, especially when the issues faced by students are legitimate and beyond their control. Yes, I know some students manipulate situations or even lie to cover up for their poor decision-making, but to act as if all students do this is absolutely wrong and unjust.

I know some teachers believe that by responding as MH's teachers responded, they are acting with equity by treating all students the same. However, these actions are not equitable. Instead, they contribute to inequity. To ignore the circumstances and backgrounds of individual students assumes that all students share the same needs for resources and support and have developed the same skills and abilities to overcome obstacles. In reality, students do not come from equal backgrounds. For MH, these responses from some of his teachers only exacerbated his struggles and pushed him down further.

Fortunately, other educators offered more meaningful support. They connected with him in engaging ways and provided inclusive curricula. These teachers played a crucial role in MH's desire to stick with school, and they supported and worked with him when he faced issues that could interfere with his classroom performance. They gave him hope, and hope turned into accomplishment.

Years after our initial meeting, MH took another class with me at a university. His development from his community college days was incredible. Ultimately, he earned a master's degree. MH earned his success every step of the way. Even with others' support, it was MH who did the work, and he was incredibly and justifiably proud of what he had achieved.

At one point, I asked MH what was important to him in his educational journey. He replied,

> I need to know my teachers care. I know it's on me to learn, but how much a teacher cares affects how I learn. I can tell some teachers really care about me as a person and want to learn from me. Those are the ones I do best with. The teachers who don't care and don't make the class interesting are a struggle for me. I don't really learn in those classes, even if I get an A in the class.

MH's story is another example of the positive impact caring teachers have on student success, and it highlights the importance of connecting with students and using Real Talk as a key behavior teachers can adopt to become more effective in the classroom.

A Sense of Belonging

Having observed that fostering a sense of belonging for students in the classroom and within school overall is pivotal in helping students of color and those from lower socioeconomic backgrounds to succeed in school, let us now consider how we can make this happen. To be clear, a sense of belonging is one crucial concept addressed through PRT, but it is not the only element that influences student success. However, I believe that cultivating a sense of belonging in the classroom is a point of entry into a broader understanding of how student experiences in the classroom impact their experiences in school overall.

To have a sense of belonging, students must feel that they matter and are "cared about, accepted, respected, valued" (Strayhorn, 2019, p. 4), and included, in the classroom. Specifically, a student's "sense of belonging has three core dimensions: cognition [thinking], affect [feelings], and behaviors [actions]" (Carter & Hurtado, 1997; see also Strayhorn, 2019, p. 80). A sense of belonging is especially important for students of color and those from lower socioeconomic backgrounds in schools where they feel marginalized (Strayhorn, 2019). Therefore, teachers and administrators must embrace creating a sense of belonging within their classrooms and schools as a priority.

Unfortunately, I have often heard "sense of belonging" used as a sound bite or buzzword in recent years. To speak of a sense of belonging with no commitment to implementing it and no understanding of how to create it within a classroom or school is damaging. When a sense of belonging is labeled as just another initiative or educational fad and not fully understood or implemented without efficacy, the entire concept is endangered and undermined. I hope that we can avoid this ominous possibility. Everyone wants to feel a sense of belonging, and it is our duty as teachers to create it for students in the classroom. A first step toward this goal is to understand what conditions are necessary for students to feel that they belong.

For students to know, instead of just guessing or hoping, that they have a connection with their teacher requires sending obvious, tangible signals to students. Through Real Talk, students know their teacher cares, respects, values, and accepts them. When a teacher is willing to be vulnerable and shares a personal story through Real Talk, this shows students the person behind the position—which is a key component of creating a sense of belonging in the classroom.

I often encounter teachers who think all they need to share in the classroom is their identity as the teacher. This approach does not achieve a connection with students. It gives the impression that the teacher has something to hide or does not see students as worthy of knowing anything more about the teacher. When a teacher uses Real Talk, this allows students to see and experience the different identities the teacher holds beyond their position of power in the classroom. For example, teachers are fathers, mothers, graduate students, sisters, brothers, athletes, musicians, and countless other things. Real Talk displays the teacher's vulnerability and concern for students as individuals. In this way, it allows students to feel safe enough to share their own personal identities, experiences, and terministic screens with the teacher. For students of color and those from lower socioeconomic backgrounds, feeling accepted, cared for, valued, and not judged is crucial in the classroom environment.

Knowing and feeling are two different things. To feel that someone cares about you requires consistent action by the other person, showing you that you matter. A feeling of belonging can happen through

Real Talk as a student becomes vulnerable with a teacher and is received with empathy and compassion. Active listening—being fully present, making eye contact, using body language focused on the student, and displaying sincere facial expressions—is an important component here. Many students have said that when I listen to them I make them feel the only thing that matters to me at that moment is what they are sharing. Asking questions to learn and understand is another key. Students will feel they have worth and value and will know you are interested in learning from and understanding them when you ask questions in response to what they share. Asking questions also shows students that their voices (and therefore their lives) matter, and it validates them as human beings.

The application of Real Talk leads students to proactively seek out teachers to connect with. This is another important aspect of helping students feel a sense of belonging. There are few things more valuable than a person's time. Teachers need to spend time with students before, after, or during class. Brief conversations, mentoring, and supporting students' extracurricular activities or personal projects are ways in which teachers can support students and show them they matter. Teacher support may also involve connecting students with appropriate resources to address issues they have shared with the teacher. In other cases, a student may simply want the teacher to give a listening ear. Just taking the time to listen, even if no subsequent action is requested or taken, can make students feel they matter. Real Talk enables these interactions to take place between students and teachers, thereby creating an environment where students feel they and their teacher belong together throughout the learning process.

Alternative lessons further strengthen students' sense of belonging by incorporating inclusion in the curriculum and how the teacher delivers it. Alternative lessons incorporate students' terministic screens, experiences, and real-life events in ways that will resonate with students. This approach allows students of color and those from lower socioeconomic backgrounds to see themselves, their experiences, or their interests reflected in the curriculum.

During one of my school presentations, a chemistry teacher shared that she tried to be inclusive with her subject matter but struggled to do so effectively. She said it was difficult for her to identify scientists of color to talk about and that making a connection from historical examples of scientists to her classroom content was problematic. This teacher was making a classic and common mistake, though with no malicious intent. Talking about diverse professionals is one way to introduce inclusive content into your classroom, but it barely scratches the surface.

As an example of a more effective approach, I worked with an incredible chemistry teacher who taught the periodic table by connecting it with languages in her classroom. She had a diverse classroom, with students from all over the world for whom English was not their first language. Through her alternative lesson, she engaged her students. She gave them a place within the curriculum by allowing them to describe the different parts of the periodic table in their first language. The lesson had additional components, too, but my main point is that this teacher found a creative way, while teaching the chemistry content, to include her students and allow them to connect themselves to the curriculum. This alternative lesson established an engaging and inclusive learning environment for her students, actively transforming the curriculum to make it more inclusive and to reinforce diverse students' sense of belonging.

Once students of color and lower socioeconomic backgrounds know and feel that they belong, as is communicated through Real Talk and alternative lessons, various positive changes happen in the classroom. One typical effect is decreased absences because, as students experience a sense of belonging in class, the classroom becomes a place where they want to be. Another common result is improved student engagement in the classroom and with the curriculum and teacher. No longer apathetic or combative about their learning process, students instead become engaged, curious, and interested in learning. They are also more likely to share their struggles in learning the material with their teacher. Armed with this understanding, the teacher can help students take positive steps forward in the learning process by reducing learning barriers. The specific manifestations among students may vary, but the one commonality is a positive behavior change, which in turn increases the likelihood that students will succeed in class. A sense of belonging transforms the learning process in the classroom into something fruitful for students rather than something they dread.

My interaction with colleagues from throughout the United States and my extensive work with students of color and those from lower socioeconomic backgrounds have helped me grasp how creating a sense of belonging in the classroom transforms student learning. As a person of color myself who grew up in severe poverty, I can confirm these insights from my own experience. To have a teacher recognize that you feel powerless and voiceless—and that you have been treated as if your life is worthless—is like being seen for the first time. This acknowledgment communicates the teacher's recognition that your dignity has been denied, that you have been judged for the burdens unfairly placed on you, and that you have been marginalized within a society that claims we are all equal. For teachers who perceive these pains in their students' lives, the problem becomes readily evident: A sense of lack of belonging leads to suffering and disengagement and thus to a lack of fulfillment and success. Teachers who use PRT build a sense of belonging in the classroom that expresses and demonstrates to students they matter, are worthy, and are capable of living fulfilled and successful lives.

A teacher once said to me, "Paul, I'm proud of you." That simple act of kindness challenged the enduring message I had heard throughout my life to that point—namely, that I was "good for nothing." It helped me feel worthy, setting the stage for me to say, "I'm proud of myself." The most successful teachers understand that "the key to raising [student success] is to recognize that teaching and learning is a relationship" (Robinson & Aronica, 2015, p. 109). PRT has embodied this understanding with sweeping success among the country's poorest-performing students and is relevant and useful for the success of all students throughout the education system.

NOTES

PART II

Implementation

Chapter 5: Implementing Real Talk in the
HEP Program   72

Chapter 6: Flexibility, Adaptability, and Effort   88

Chapter 7: Terministic Screens, Alternative
Lessons, and Real Talk Discussions   96

Chapter 8: Implementing Real Talk in
Any Classroom   109

5 Implementing Real Talk in the HEP Program

In Chapter 2, the foundations of PRT were discussed: dialogue based on Freire's *Pedagogy of the Oppressed*, S.C.R.E.A.M., Meyer's characteristics of successful teachers, terministic screens, alternative lessons, flexibility, and Real Talk discussions. However, knowing what the pieces are and knowing how to put them all together are not the same. Just as we need to see the picture of the completed puzzle to put the individual pieces in the right positions, so too do we need to understand the overall purpose and components of a pedagogy before we can put them together to help students achieve academic success.

In the next three chapters, we will look at the details of the implementation of PRT. This chapter details the implementation of dialogue, relating to students, structure, clarity, redundancy, enthusiasm, appropriate pace, and maximized engagement. Chapter 6 discusses flexibility, adaptability, and effort. The most powerful component, Real Talk discussions, is the topic of Chapter 7. Because some of the concepts within the pieces are similar, determining if something in the implementation of the pedagogy is an example of flexibility or adaptability, for example, is moot. I've combined such concepts in these chapters to give a true portrayal of how PRT is implemented in classrooms.

In addition, as with any pedagogy, implementation is an ongoing process. As you gain a better understanding of PRT, you will refine your skill in implementing the components. With each semester, you will establish connections with your students faster. This is crucial in the arena of education because we do not have the luxury of time.

Dialogue

Dialogue is embedded throughout PRT. It cannot really be separated from all of the other components because it is contained within each to some extent. Thus, dialogue flows throughout the structure of class over the course of the semester.

Respect is a baseline objective in the pedagogy. The focus of class is to get to know students thoroughly to maximize their engagement in the learning process. To accomplish this, you must treat and respect students as human beings yet always maintain your professional position as the teacher. Never try to control or force students to learn. Rather, include and integrate them as part of their own learning experiences. As you and the students develop mutual levels of respect, they will feel that your desire to hear their opinions and understand their backgrounds is genuine. This, in turn, will lead to drastic increases in their interest in learning. Teachers of any background can use mutual respect as a starting point for their instructional focus.

During the first week of class with the students, I did not overwhelm them with work or assignments. Instead, we began with dialogue in the classroom. On the first day, I introduced myself as a person: my background, where I was from, and my interests outside of the classroom. After my initial introduction, I turned the floor over to the students and asked them to tell me where they were from and a bit about their backgrounds and interests outside of class. Instead of focusing on school, we began establishing a mutual dialogue in the classroom. As more and more students spoke up, I eventually transitioned our discussion to school and the purpose it serves within our lives.

I usually led the dialogue in the beginning stages of class to build trust and student confidence. I began by first giving them insights into my life and connecting it to the classroom we shared. I explained that education was something that had allowed me to take myself from the gutters of Los Angeles to the faculty offices of a midwestern university. I explained that all the classes I had ever taken had never suggested incorporating my life experiences into the classroom, so our classroom would be different. There, everyone's stories would be used to make sense of why we were learning the things we needed to know to pass the reading and writing components of the GED.

Slowly but surely during the first week of class, more and more students shared about their lives and what education meant to them. The dialogue introduced the students' lives into the classroom, as well as mine, as we began to learn from one another. I integrated the problems into what they learned to add relevance to their learning. Ultimately, I introduced the "real world" into the often mundane world of the classroom.

I was open with my students, acknowledging the information I continually learned from them and often thanking them for teaching me something new. I was never the "all-knowing" teacher. Instead, I was their teacher who knew some things but not all things. Their excitement in knowing they taught me as much as I taught them created an electric atmosphere in which the students and I engaged in learning during the time we spent in the classroom. Thus, dialogue impacted the students in a manner that made them react positively in class. Although I gained some insights into their terministic screens and lives—Real Talk served as the most powerful approach to gain in-depth understandings of these things—I empowered them to become part of the teaching process during class.

Relating to Students

Befriending students is not the intent or the focus of this approach. In PRT, the aim is to find ways to relate the curriculum to the students' terministic screens or experiences. The high school equivalency program (HEP) associate director had strongly emphasized connecting with our students to generate success in the classroom, stating in one of our first meetings, "If you cannot connect with these students, then you will not be successful with them." The recruiter had reinforced this message. Thus, relating to my students could not be merely a matter of having some similarities with them. It had to be derived through developing rapport with them by "talking with them, laughing with them, counseling them, [and] reaching them on their own level" (Meyer, 1968, p. 3).

The associate director of HEP told me that one of the biggest issues teachers faced was relating to their students and finding ways to connect the material in meaningful ways to their lives: "I can't stress it enough. You must find a way to relate with students in order to connect with them. Once you connect, you will see; they will want to learn." Her urgency and sincerity were apparent when we spoke, but I noted that it was up to each instructor to discover the methods needed to make learning meaningful for his or her students.

The recruiter also routinely engaged me in conversations regarding students. As he prepared me for my first semester, he echoed this now-familiar message:

> Paul, you must connect with them because, if you do not, they will not be receptive to you or what you are trying to teach them. . . . I wish I could tell you how to do it, but I can't. It will be a difficult task, and I pray to God that you will find a way and be successful with all of our students. Other teachers have managed to find connections with students, so I have faith that you can too.

However, it is a daunting task to identify ways to connect with students or to relate to them before even meeting them. At times, I felt overwhelmed, privately admitting feelings of defeat after discussions with colleagues regarding our students.

I typically discovered the students' personal issues and made connections during class discussions. I then used that information as a tool to create recognizable links to the curriculum. Rather than hinder or discourage discussion of these issues, I used them as teachable moments, as one of my students described during the interviews:

> His class connects with us, and I just feel like he really understands my pain and helps me learn from it. He has been there before in our shoes, and he has made it out of the gutter. He knows how to take his past and my past experiences and turn them into some real-ass lessons in the classroom.

Although my students and I were very different and had not shared the exact same experiences, I emphasized engaging my students in open dialogue and, as a result, learned things about them. As I learned about them, I could see how our lives paralleled in so many ways. It was not about having the exact same experiences when it came to relating to my students; rather, it was understanding that, as human beings, we share common struggles. We may experience them in different ways, but we constantly seek out ways to move onward and upward. Relating to my students was not about changing who I was or attempting to be more like them. Rather, it was about tearing down the social constructions that kept us apart. Relating to my students required a combination of willingness, transparency, eagerness, honesty, and authenticity while maintaining my position as their guide (teacher) to overcome the obstacles (GED subjects) they faced. As they recognized these things within my approach to working with them, we began to relate to each other in a meaningful manner. Ultimately, Real Talk and the other components of the pedagogy facilitated my relating to my students by making it much easier and systematic yet allowing me to remain authentic.

Structure

Structure for my classes was based on two things: the general structure of the HEP program and the S.C.R.E.A.M. variables. Structure for students came by way of class schedules, which provided a level of consistency that many of them were not accustomed to within their personal lives. Within the HEP program, they attended classes following consistent daily and weekly schedules that they could rely on, day in and day out. They could also count on their same group of teachers being there for them throughout the entire semester. The classroom structure I created also gave them an opportunity to escape the volatility and lack of clear expectations many of my students encountered in their everyday lives.

The curriculum for the GED classes was based on the Steck-Vaughn GED textbook series (Northcutt et al., 2002) and, thus, remained virtually the same each semester. This series provided students with clear expectations for coursework structure and style. Although individual teachers added supplemental materials and activities to their classes, the foundation of the curriculum remained consistent across all subjects.

In addition to the schedule and materials used, I established structure within my class by creating basic routines. During the first five to 10 minutes of every class, we discussed what was happening in my students' lives and in my life (always using discretion). Students became accustomed to having time for personal talk at the beginning of every class before delving into our work. This routine served a very powerful purpose: It removed the stress of being in a classroom by allowing students to "get things off their chests." Sometimes, we smiled and laughed; on other occasions, we simply took time to know one another beyond our classroom roles. Thus, the classroom became a far less stressful place for my students. When the time allotted for these personal discussions ended, I always turned our attention back to the curriculum for the day. The small amount of time dedicated to speaking before we began working paid large dividends because the students were more focused on their schoolwork for the remainder of the class.

Another routine in my class structure was the writing of a paper every Monday. Weekends were when HEP students, like so many other students, simply forgot about school. To collect any work from them or to have them engage in work on Mondays was typically a challenging task. However, because the students were typically excited to share their weekend endeavors, I used that effectively to get them to write, creating Monday papers. These were papers students wrote about what they had done over the weekend. They knew my expectation was for them to have their papers written for the start of class on Monday. Many of these students were scared of writing and struggled to write even a paragraph. By having them tell me about their weekends, I broke through their fear of writing and slowly but surely taught them the rules they needed to become better, more competent writers. They also appreciated the fact that I read their papers and at times spoke to them or asked them questions about the things they wrote. Because they felt valued in class, over time, they wrote more and more as they became comfortable with the writing process. Just as they shared their weekends with me, I, in turn, shared mine with them, using discretion at all times. The students felt it was only fair that I do so because they were sharing with me.

Teachers can structure their classes in a variety of ways. The key is to be consistent and to allow student feedback. Once we establish routines in our classrooms, our students will regard them as classroom norms. Such norms minimize the need for constant reminders about what they need to do and reduce the occasions on which students tell us that they forgot their homework assignments. When we incorporate our students into the structure of our classrooms, they are more likely to accept what we expect of them, diminishing their level of resistance and increasing consistency in the classroom.

Clarity

Clarity is an important aspect of any classroom. Students echo how important it is for them to understand the material, understand me, and know my expectations of them. Thus, usage and vocabulary are important dimensions of clarity. You should seldom use complex language or vocabulary in class, but when you do, take the time to teach the meaning and proper use of the language you use. Therefore, you will use a combination of the students' vernacular and yours during your discussions in class, establishing a linguistic middle ground to ensure clarity.

Clarity also involves being honest with students about who you are not only as an instructor but also as a person. For example, when I found myself missing Los Angeles, I shared with my students that I was having a bad day because I felt homesick and might not be as engaging as I usually was. At times, my honesty with my students surprised my colleagues, who felt I was too open about myself. However, through this openness, I began developing relationships with my students. Those relationships stimulated students' engagement in their learning. Because of my sharing of myself, my students felt more connected, wanted to listen, and shared more about themselves and their experiences during our discussions in class.

Of more importance, clarity includes making sure students understand your expectations of them in class. Especially focus on getting students to understand that their actions have consequences and that the people around them throughout their lives, including school, may respond to their actions in different ways. Many students are not accustomed to taking responsibility for their actions, even in situations when they clearly committed inappropriate acts or broke rules or laws. In many cases, it is because they have been routinely treated unfairly or falsely accused of things both in school and in their personal lives, making it difficult to admit to anything.

Instead, they learn to obfuscate their actions and blame others and have developed expert-level tactics to deflect responsibility, all to protect themselves. Because many students at-promise expect to be disrespected and blamed, they take a defensive or standoffish stance toward educators. What has become a survival mechanism for these students ultimately works against them in the classroom. Even when they are approached by well-intentioned teachers who have the students' best interests in mind, students at-promise tend to be defensive. Therefore, establishing clarity was a crucial component in breaking the defense tactics my HEP students used in the classroom.

Many HEP students, like many other students at-promise, also tend to view teachers and administrators as people who discipline them unfairly. Although some teachers and administrators do unfairly target students at-promise, assuming all educators unfairly stigmatize students at-promise is inaccurate. The point of sharing this with the class was to ensure they clearly understood the consequences of their actions in the classroom. This included understanding that both teacher and program responses to their actions were not personal attacks but reactions to the students' actions. Thus, I defused the students' belief that they were being personally attacked when disciplinary issues arose. Through the clarity we established, students began to take responsibility for their actions instead of becoming defensive or resistant, or interpreting people's responses as personal attacks. We also established a clear understanding of the role their actions had in their success.

By establishing clarity in the classroom, I effectively established a better line of communication with my students, avoiding many misunderstandings and unnecessary problems. The students learned to expect that I would give them my best effort in teaching to help them pass the GED, and that I would be fair with them. Clarity also prevented the students from "reading between lines"; there were no "gray areas" they could manipulate, even though some of these students were experts in finding loopholes. As a result of clarity, there was little room for misinterpreting anything we discussed in class. Ultimately, clarity was an effective tool in bringing the students and me closer together in a manner that further strengthened our success. Through clarity, the students respected and accepted the expectations we had established.

Redundancy

As stated in Chapter 2, redundancy includes repetition, reiteration, and reinforcement. I practiced redundancy in the classroom through multiple approaches to teach my students the core academic concepts and to support the learning style of each student. As Mojica (2006), noted, reiteration occurs "where the interpretation of some element in the discourse is dependent of another . . . whether they have the same referent or whether a referential relationship exists between them" (p. 110). Therefore, I maintained the interconnectedness between each lesson and the core academic concepts. As one student noted, "We be watching video clips on YouTube, cool documentaries, we be reading song lyrics from 2Pac, and this man be tying everything to the GED stuff" (Mojica, 2006). Thus, the concepts from the GED were taught numerous times but in different formats, allowing the students to understand the concepts in a variety of ways.

I presented every concept in a multitude of ways and, when possible, also tried to combine concepts in lessons (e.g., making inferences, identifying style and tone, and drawing conclusions). But whether I was teaching one concept or many, the lesson was usually short, concise, and engaging, designed to draw my students into the learning process.

One concept that required redundancy for students to learn was making inferences. The Steck-Vaughn book (Northcutt et al., 2002) gave two statements on making inferences. The first stated, "Sometimes when you read nonfiction, facts are only implied or suggested. In such cases you must figure out what the author is saying by using both stated and suggested information. This skill is called making inferences" (Northcutt et al., 2002, p. 60). The second was, "Making an inference [means] using stated and suggested information to figure out an unstated idea" (Northcutt et al., 2002, p. 60). Although these are good, the statements did not resonate with my students. These statements reflect the vernacular of the mainstream middle class. As such, they exclude entire groups of people who might easily comprehend the concept if it were explained in a different vernacular. My students needed an explanation that resonated with them, something more relevant to them that still maintained the academic meaning of making inferences.

In my first alternative lesson, I asked students how they could tell someone they cared about was mad at them without being explicitly told. This immediately connected the lesson with their personal lives. Students' responses to my question varied:

- "Yeah, I can tell because they act differently."
- "Because the way they talk to me changes, so I know something is wrong."
- "It's hard to explain, but I can figure it out by the little things that change in them."

After they shared their views, I explained that although they had no solid evidence, they put the information they did have together to come up with their determination and that, in doing so, they were making inferences. Most of my students grasped the concept after this short exercise; then we moved on to other examples of the same concept.

I also used YouTube, DVDs, and video streaming to help my students understand concepts because movie scenes can be powerful tools to reinforce concepts. Before showing a scene, I always asked the class who had seen the particular movie I hoped to use. If the majority of the class had not, I felt the clip was new enough and fresh enough to stimulate learning. However, I always had scenes from other movies ready to use in case too many students in class had already watched my first choice. I did not provide my students with any background material or the story line. Instead, I asked students to be attentive as they watched the clip and to write down what they felt the people in the scene were feeling or thinking and what they thought the movie could potentially be about. I typically selected emotional scenes that helped my students feel what was happening to the characters in the particular clip.

One clip I used in class to teach making inferences was from *Braveheart* (1995), starring Mel Gibson. I showed 10 minutes from a scene in which William Wallace, accused of treason, is tortured. Wallace is asked to "fall to your knees now. Declare yourself the king's loyal subject and beg his mercy and you shall have it" (Scene 20). The consequence Wallace must face for not begging for mercy is being tortured before he is executed. In the scene, some people connected to Wallace are in the audience that has gathered to watch him die. The clip contains little dialogue.

After showing the scene, I asked the class a series of questions to help them extract inferences from the clip:

- What do you think William Wallace was thinking or feeling besides the obvious physical pain?
- What were his two friends in the crowd thinking or feeling based on what you saw?

I used similar questions, which might vary from class to class, to induce class discussions to reinforce their skills in making inferences to show students how they decipher things without fully knowing the facts or all of the information. When appropriate, I also used the clip to reinforce other concepts. In the case of this particular clip, I could incorporate the concepts of identifying style and tone, drawing conclusions, identifying plot, and analyzing character.

I then assigned homework that reiterated the concepts. In this case, the assignment was to write down a few verses from a song that the students felt had powerful meaning. They were not to include the name of the song in their lyrics. That way, students had to make inferences based only on the information provided. I collected the lyrics the next day, mixed them up, and redistributed them, making sure each student received a new set of lyrics. After the students read their lyrics, I randomly selected students to share the lyrics and to explain what they could infer from what they had been provided. The students typically had fun with this assignment and were comfortable sharing their thoughts. In addition, they were simultaneously learning and practicing the concept of making inferences.

As the final step, students completed the few exercises and mini tests provided in the Steck-Vaughn book to make sure they grasped the meaning of the concept. I also integrated other mini tests from GED prep resources to make sure my students applied the concept consistently in a variety of materials.

Although such lessons seem tedious when written out, teachers can execute them quite effectively within the time constraints of most class periods. This is possible because the overall pedagogy helps teachers eliminate distractions and disciplinary referrals within class.

Enthusiasm

The most difficult and exhausting aspect of the structure for me personally was enthusiasm. Although I was genuinely happy to be in the classroom with my students, sometimes it was difficult to conjure true outward enthusiasm. Still, I attempted to arrive to every class with an enthusiastic attitude. On a typical day in my class, I greeted students at the door or acknowledged them as they walked into class and found seats. I did not pretend to be happy or excited but focused my enthusiasm with students on the everyday preparation for class and on getting them closer to passing the GED. I focused their goal of passing the GED into a form of "beating their adversary" to overcome an obstacle within their lives. The basis for my enthusiasm was the personal gains I knew they could achieve when they used education as an avenue for success. My students accepted this as a legitimate reason to be enthused about coming to class and about looking forward to taking their exams. This enthusiasm also allowed students to view me as their ally in their quest to overcome a standardized test that, like so many other exams in their lives, had proven to be an obstacle for them.

When presenting material to the students, I tried to make the lessons interesting by mixing them in with other concepts. I showed students my excitement in the ways I spoke about the material and connected it to them and their passing the GED. I was eager to answer student questions; when they asked questions, I exemplified that excitement to help minimize their fears. This fostered a fun learning environment for students while they were engaged with the core concepts needed to pass the GED exams.

On a more individual level, I showed my enthusiasm to my students through my authentic interest in what they had to say and what they were willing to share. I listened intently in our conversations, giving them feedback when appropriate. The HEP students, like so many students at-promise, were not accustomed to having a voice in society; they were used to having their voice ignored because others were unwilling to listen to what they had to say. As enthusiastic as I was to listen to them, they were even more excited to share. They enjoyed sharing what they had to say with a person who was willing to listen and was not judging them in the process. Understand that my students were not my friends; the line between student and teacher was never blurred. I simply treated my students as human beings. I was excited to learn more about them, which helped me better prepare them to overcome the obstacle that stood before us.

However, some days I had difficulty being enthusiastic because I did not feel well physically, emotionally, or mentally. On those days, because I was authentic with my students, they noticed my lack of enthusiasm and inquired whether I was okay. This was a positive and exciting experience for me because these students typically did not spend time or energy worrying about how their teachers felt. Because I wanted to be genuine with them, I did not force my enthusiasm in the classroom. Doing so would have had negative consequences. My students were experts in seeing through superficial behavior. For them, reading people was a survival mechanism. They respected teachers who showed that they were not emotionless robots in the classroom but rather people who had good days and bad days just like them. Thus, establishing genuine enthusiasm with my students was more important and effective than being inauthentic. Over time, the norm in my classes was that, as a group, we were enthusiastic in working with one another five days a week until the day they took their exams.

Appropriate Pace

Determining appropriate pace is a task that requires constant attention throughout every semester. The first week of class, I focused on three main activities to determine appropriate pace: (1) asking the students about the pace of the class, (2) having students write about the class pace, and (3) giving students weekly exams or assessments to monitor the pace of student learning. Every day, I spoke individually with at least two students for a few minutes before and after class about the pace of the class. Speaking to students is extremely valuable. As their comfort level with me grew, they openly discussed their difficulties with the material we'd covered and what they had comprehended. Through these conversations, students unknowingly afforded me tremendous insight into what style of learning was most effective for them and how they comprehended the material. With this information, I altered my teaching to impact more students and to establish a consistent pace for the entire class. These discussions also served as unexpected sources of information about other students and more opportunities to achieve an appropriate pace for class.

Some students were not as willing as others to share their frustrations or lack of understanding because they were embarrassed or did not want to show me any sign of weakness. However, other students spoke on behalf of their peers as they told me how they were helping other students during personal time. Through these conversations, I gained the information I needed to address the difficulties these quieter students faced in the curriculum. I also learned which students were more advanced in the curriculum from those offering help to those struggling. I often had the more advanced students answer questions from their points of view, thus offering different viewpoints of the concepts being taught in class. This not only helped the rest of the students but also solidified the understanding of the advanced students.

I used a weekly writing assignment—a one-page reflection on class progress—to determine if the pace was too fast or too slow. This gave my students an avenue to vent their frustrations regarding concepts, my teaching, supplemental material used, or any other obstacle that inhibited them from comprehending what was being taught. Before and after every written reflection, I reminded the class that my ability to teach them would only improve with their honesty, that my manner of teaching was not perfect, and that only with their help could I effectively prepare them to pass the GED. Sharing this was an important component in empowering them to become part of the teaching process and in validating their views in the classroom. As students became accustomed to writing, their comfort level increased. In turn, they became more candid in their reflections, which allowed me to solidify the most suitable pace for the class. By the third week of the semester, student responses about the class pace were fairly consistent.

My assessments were also designed to guide instruction. Through them, I could identify each student's strengths and weaknesses, rate of learning, and ways in which each student could best demonstrate that learning (Meisels et al., 2002). In addition, all students were required to participate in weekly official GED practice-testing sessions. The mini tests and quizzes taken in class were directly created from GED practice questions and were timed to help students become comfortable with the time constraints of the official GED. These assessments and methods, combined with daily discussions with students during and after class, helped me to determine the appropriate pace of the class. Eventually, the class moved at a swift yet comfortable pace, allowing us not to feel pressured by time constraints.

Maximized Engagement

Although the administrators strongly emphasized engaging our students in class, the idea of maximizing engagement was easier than its implementation in my classes. I did much self-reflecting concerning how I engaged the class and how I could improve this engagement throughout the semester. I found that connecting concepts through both my students' life stories and my own was key in engaging my students. For example, when discussing symbolism, I provided examples of symbols from my life. I shared that to me a negative symbol was police officers or any type of law enforcement because, as a young man, I had negative experiences with them. When I was growing up, law enforcement symbolized corruption; they were bad people, not the good guys they represented for most other members of society (see Appendices E and I for additional examples). I then asked my students to share symbols from their lives. The students were eager to share their stories and, without realizing it, became intensely engaged in the class. This process fostered the development of positive rapport with the students as well.

Maximized engagement turns the classroom into a place in which students feel free: free of judgment and harsh punishments because of their perspectives and experiences, and free to engage in their own learning processes. Class was focused solely on neither the students' views of the world nor their development toward passing the GED exams. Rather, maximized engagement included stimulating students to share parts of themselves and to learn about others and about me in class. Thus, engaging students became a surprisingly trouble-free, enjoyable task.

Two activities that were particularly successful in maximizing engagement were Monday discussions and student presentations. Every Monday during each semester, my first class began with a discussion about each student's weekend activities. Because I inquired about their weekends, the students began inquiring about mine as well. Students were also assigned presentations about their favorite songs (limited to two songs per student). Students were typically very excited to share what they titled "a piece of myself" with the class. After playing their songs to the class, the students explained the meanings of their songs and their importance to them. I paid close attention during these presentations, provided positive feedback, and tried to help the students express themselves when they struggled.

I also asked questions about the presentations based on core connections to the curriculum. The class covered concepts such as interpreting theme, interpreting figurative language, making inferences, finding the main idea, restating information, identifying style and tone, and recognizing author's point of view. Students had to express their opinions, feelings, and points of view, which were also restated within the lessons. As with all of the assignments, the presentations led to a writing exercise that allowed students to implement aspects of their last four textbook units (sentence structure, organization, usage, and mechanics). The presentations also strengthened the overall rapport between the students and me, as one student noted: "I don't feel judged. You listen to me and you respect me. This is all I have ever asked from people and teachers."

Maximized engagement was not simply a matter of students doing work in my class or contributing to class discussions. It was about students feeling that our time together was not simply *a* class or the *teacher's* class but *our* class. They took ownership and had a sense of belonging that was established by asking for their input about how continually to improve the class (e.g., make things more interesting, improve lessons, incorporate new material). Many students made suggestions to improve the class; I not only listened but also, in many instances, implemented their suggestions. Although students typically noticed when their ideas and comments were used in class, I also acknowledged and thanked them for the suggestions during class. Acknowledgement kept students engaged in the class because they became part of the evolution of our class. Through their ideas for improvement, students also became more invested in their own learning process. Thus, student input is an intricate part of class; their insight needs to be respected, whether or not we agree with them.

Our position in class is not to demean or belittle their ideas. We are there to help students develop critically by expanding on their ideas to afford them educated and more encompassing perspectives. As they share their views, contribute to lessons, answer questions, and help others, they will develop a sense of belonging in class. Many students will feel valued because they will sense that you authentically value them. Your class should be a place where students belong rather than just a place where they take up space and waste time. For many students at-promise, having a place where they feel they belong and where they are not viewed or treated as burdens contributes to their willingness to learn and keeps them engaged in the classroom.

Through maximizing engagement, students become an intricate part of the learning process rather than simply audience members who absorb everything a teacher presents. Students will spend their time and energy being engaged in what is discussed and shared, all of which will ultimately connect back to what is being taught in the classroom. Students will dedicate very little energy to disrupting the learning process, and they won't be distracted. Because they will remain engaged, students will not count the seconds they are in class; the time spent in class will simply breeze by—a major victory considering that students at risk would normally complain about the length of the class and about their boredom or lack of interest. Thus, maximizing engagement is critical to the ultimate success of our students.

6 Flexibility, Adaptability, and Effort

Relating to students and teaching students a set curriculum using personal connections are two completely different things. I had to seize on my students' eagerness to learn by integrating the curriculum they needed to pass the GED. As I applied the concepts of my PRT, I truly grasped the necessity of S.C.R.E.A.M. combined with flexibility, or S.C.R.E.A.M.+F. I also realized that flexibility and Meyer's characteristics of a successful teacher, which I define as adaptability, were similar. In this chapter, I discuss the characteristics of flexibility, adaptability, and effort and their importance to student success.

Before beginning my first semester at the MSU HEP, the recruiter told me that I needed to "do something different" from the kinds of things the students had done in their previous schools if I was going to help them succeed. The assistant director cautioned me that "entirely traditional approaches toward these students will not be effective." I struggled to get my students to learn the material. Even though they were engaged and well behaved in the classroom and I had established a positive rapport with them, they were not learning as much as they needed to learn in the short time they had to prepare for the GED.

I became frustrated and, in a few instances, even lashed out at the class. On one occasion when that happened, my students asked me what was wrong and why I was acting differently. I shared my frustration with them regarding their scores and blamed myself because I knew they were working hard. The students were pleasantly shocked when they heard me give them recognition for their hard work, but they felt I was being too hard on myself. In class that day, we brainstormed what I could do to help them improve their grades. We finished the day with no clear solution but had latched on to the idea of being flexible in the classroom.

Flexibility

That night, I altered my lesson plans to create a clearer way for students to understand and learn the concepts in the class. I decided to teach some lessons through games, allowing students to work and compete in groups. I also had students participate at the chalkboard to teach and share their ideas and understanding of the concepts and skills they were learning. We went from a predominantly lecture- and individual-based learning environment to one that encompassed working in groups of various sizes, students teaching concepts (with assistance when needed), and participating in more interactive activities such as games to reinforce learning. To a visitor, the class might have seemed chaotic, but it was an active, student-engaged, student-centered learning environment. After only two weeks, I noticed that students were scoring better on assessments and that class averages were rising considerably. This trend of rising scores continued throughout the semester as I continued to change and modify lessons.

An example of a modified lesson is allowing a student to join instruction based on his or her own experiences. For instance, one of my quieter but engaged students asked me if he could explain to everyone what sentence structure meant and why it was needed. I gladly handed him the floor and sat with the rest of the class, paying close attention to his lesson. The student introduced the idea of "structure in the hood." Everyone knew and understood the rules or structure of their neighborhoods without having to think twice. He expanded the idea, saying that in their own neighborhoods, they knew where it was safe, where the violence happened, where the drugs were, where the police hid, and where the different people hung out. When their neighborhood structure was "off," they could tell or identify it without having to ask anyone. He reminded the class that although outsiders thought their neighborhoods were crazy, the students could make sense of them because they knew the structure. If they did not know the structure of their hoods, they might be not only lost but also in danger at times.

The student transitioned from neighborhood structure to sentence structure, explaining that sentences make sense when students write them or read them and recognize errors in them. He then wrote four sentences on the chalkboard and asked the class to determine if something was wrong with each sentence and, if so, to point out what was wrong. To others, the hood example might have been confusing or meaningless, but to his peers, the lesson made perfect sense. The students were intrigued and receptive, and they participated. Toward the end of his lesson, I joined him to expand further on sentence structure. Thus, through flexibility, this young man became empowered, leading and teaching the entire class.

Although teachers might think such changes will take an abundance of effort or time, a few days making alterations can make a difference. Besides the improvement in test scores, students also provided ideas for modifications, which reduced my preparation time and the time spent on discipline within the classroom.

Flexibility is also crucial when something that works with one group of students does not work with another. I had established Real Talk sessions focused on experiences of racism and class discrimination. The majority of the students had revealed fairly consistent terministic screens, and I had developed an effective structure with which I was comfortable. However, when I tried to apply these lessons with a new class, I did not receive a positive response. The new set of students divulged perspectives that revealed discriminatory views of other racial and social class groups rather than personal experiences. Thus, my previous structural focus was irrelevant and ineffective. I restructured many of my lessons, Real Talk discussions, and reviews to emphasize the creation and implementation of stereotypes and the negative impact they have on people. The students were much more receptive to the new lessons and became more involved with them, making it easier for me to teach this particular group of students.

Flexibility also means keeping the internal structure of the class varied. Within a one-hour class, keep students engaged by changing the lessons, games, lectures, and type of work performed in class. Although I followed a general structure, the daily activities in my classes were different to ensure students were not bored or "shut off" to what I was teaching them.

Because students will not always be receptive to every lesson as planned, try not to approach a class one-dimensionally. For example, when you are delivering any lesson in the classroom, you must pay close attention to your students' receptiveness and needs. If students are not interested in what you are teaching them, be willing to change the examples or lessons you are using. Ask students if they are interested in what you are teaching them and, if not, why they are not interested and how you could make it better for them. Often, we as educators feel an obligation to have to be "right" or know all the answers, but we can't and don't know everything. In fact, there will be times that students are better versed in something than the teachers. By openly inviting students to contribute, you are allowing yourself to be flexible and amenable to shifting what you are teaching in "real time," putting your students' needs in the forefront of your teaching.

Incorporate things in your classroom that push you beyond your comfort zone. We all have specific styles in which we deliver our lessons, and we typically stay within that style. But at times, our students need us to push ourselves for the sake of their learning. For example, if you are a serious teacher who seldom laughs, perhaps you would be willing to try a day where you are lighthearted and funny in class. Or if you are a teacher who is always making students laugh, perhaps you take a day where you focus on things in a more serious manner. The point is to remain flexible on all fronts and push yourself to be multidimensional.

In the early stages of incorporating flexibility, I was nervous with the changes I made because I felt that I was going against the norm of what other teachers do with students. However, I quickly realized that it was not about doing what other teachers were doing but about doing what was effective for my students. I felt the most pressure when I realized that students were losing interest in my lesson and that their focus on what I was teaching diminished. Almost instinctively, because I did not want to admit defeat or ineffectiveness, I found myself imposing ineffective and boring lessons on my students. It is difficult for teachers to accept that we are not effective at times in the classroom; it is simply easier for us to blame the students. I learned that to try something different, I had to be flexible and honest with my students. The sheer honesty and willingness to find something else was more effective and paid tremendous dividends not only in students' test scores but also in our relationship in the classroom.

Adaptability

Adaptability requires attention to your students' needs and to their levels of understanding. It is important to incorporate appropriate assessments throughout the semester. Just listening to the students during our class lessons is one way to assess their learning. For example, during an alternative lesson on making inferences, comparing, and contrasting, my students struggled to grasp the concepts. I led our discussion toward students' dream cars and had the students do an in-class side-by-side evaluation of three of these cars. I had already extracted the three most popular dream cars from previous Real Talk discussions we had had in class. Students used the internet to gather information about prices, engines, and performance; descriptions of the interiors and exteriors; lists of safety features; and reviews by both experts and car owners. They also found photos of each car. They presented the information via the overhead projector and then proceeded to evaluate the three cars.

This type of alternative lesson engaged the students; subtly reinforced the concepts of inference, comparison, and contrast introduced in the initial lesson; and helped eliminate their confusion about those concepts. This lesson did not require hours of preplanning. The students had already given me the information about their dream cars through our Real Talk discussions. The internet resources were instantly available. This impromptu lesson took little more than listening to student responses to recognize their confusion and the ineffectiveness of my planned lesson and a willingness to be flexible and change the lesson context while still delivering the necessary lesson content.

Adaptability is also key in meeting the needs of different classes. Don't force students to adapt to rigid lesson plans. Instead, if needed, adapt lessons and ideas from one semester to the next and from one group of students to the next. I found that allowing students to have a voice in the class helped me identify what was successful with them and what was not; then I tweaked the lessons to ensure student success. This ultimately allowed me to teach the students the material and be within Meyer's successful teacher characteristic of being able to teach the students. Although flexibility and adaptability are a focus of my pedagogy, I also try to instill in my students that these are characteristics they need to work with different types of instructors, employers, and coworkers.

Students are extremely diverse in their personalities, styles, and interests. We as teachers must adapt to the different personalities and groups of people that our students represent. Although I saw many teachers attempt to force, intimidate, punish, or ignore students who were not the type of person with whom they felt they could relate, it is far better to adapt to your students. I tried not to superimpose my views or interests on my students or make assumptions about them. Instead, I listened actively to gain insight into who they were as people. I adapted to students who at first glance seemed annoying and irritating or who were standoffish or aggressive toward me. I attempted to build positive relationships through my pedagogy with students and learn about their personalities. I was able to connect with them and build positive relationships wherein they trusted me and I trusted them by using Real Talk. Thus, I connected with a multitude of students—including the young, openly gay man in my class who felt he couldn't trust heterosexual men and the angry woman who hated men because of tragic negative experiences throughout her life—rather than only a select group that were most similar to me as a person.

At times, perhaps unconsciously, we tend to connect with students with whom we can talk easily and to alienate those who challenge us when we speak with them. We may not be able to connect with students at-promise as easily as we do with others. There are a multitude of reasons why this is so. Students at-promise might distrust authority figures because of their negative personal experiences with them or because of substance abuse. They might be reclusive due to bullying or other negative experiences, have become cynical toward teachers and the education system, be apathetic due to their life experiences, or feel bored with and disengaged from school, among other reasons. But it is for these same reasons that it is absolutely crucial that we tirelessly attempt to authentically connect and engage these students, serve as a source of empowerment for them, offer them a safe place within our classroom, and potentially find solutions to their struggles for them to become successful not only in school but also in their lives. It is the students that need us the most that will push us away the most. Don't let this be a deterrent; instead, let it be a signal for us to make sure we are committed to adapt in the necessary ways to make sure we are successful with all of our students.

Effort

Effort in teaching students refers not to completing the bare minimum with students, but to being truly available at times that are convenient for the students. Spending extra time with students can be a better use of time than preplanning or disciplining. Make time to work with students who have questions about classwork or to discuss personal issues affecting their performance in class. Meet with students before class, during class, and after class. The extra time spent with students is extremely useful in creating connections, making your job easier and the classroom more enjoyable for all.

Taking some extra time with students is often minimal compared with the powerful results that it yields. Often, questions about the class that the students thought were difficult or overwhelming were simple for me to answer, given my knowledge of the curriculum and my professional preparation. Thus, I could quickly and effectively work one-on-one with my students. Their confidence increased while their doubts decreased. One student commented, "[Paul] has always made time for me, and I really appreciate that. It makes me work harder in his class." If you are unable to meet with students, use clear and honest communication to avoid offending them. For example, instead of telling students that I was busy, I explained the specific reason I could not meet with them. This was simple and subtle but greatly appreciated by my students, who shared how different it was to meet a teacher who made time for them. Thus, over the course of our 12 weeks together, these small investments of time paid tremendous dividends in positive relationships.

In PRT, effort and involvement are crucial to student success. In many cases, students viewed the time I spent with them as a sign of respect and caring. These feelings, in turn, inspired many of my students to put forth more effort in their studies and preparation to pass the GED. When they saw they were continually improving in their assignments, exams, understanding of material, and overall critical development, it felt like a personal victory.

Many people think that teachers have a positive attitude toward all of their students, but I have found that this is not always true. We assume that people become teachers because they like students. However, as one teacher posed, how do we maintain a genuine positive attitude with a group of challenging students at-promise who seemingly do not want to learn and have no regard for their teachers? It can be extraordinarily difficult to maintain a positive attitude toward some students at-promise, given their involvement in self-destructive behavior inside and outside of the classroom. It is important to acknowledge their challenging behavior and discuss its consequences rather than ignore their problems. Ignoring issues only exacerbates them. I was determined to maintain a positive attitude and to make every student aware that I believed in their ability to turn their lives in a more positive direction. Know about existing resources (e.g., counseling, substance abuse programs, gang prevention programs, women's shelters) to help them deal with the issues they face, but don't impose these things on your students. Awareness and positive feedback help students see their lives as hopeful.

It's critical to maintain a genuine positive attitude toward the work that the students do in class. My students often became frustrated with their work because, historically, many of them were not successful students. It frustrated them that they did not grow by leaps and bounds in the classroom. They blamed themselves, referred to themselves as stupid, became frustrated and lashed out at others, accused the lessons they were learning of being worthless, and even blamed me for not helping them enough. Although I could easily have become cynical and disregarded them, I understood that my students were no different from other people who, when they grow frustrated or do not understand something, become difficult to be around. My frustration grew as theirs did, but rather than lash out, I simply smiled and told them things were going to be okay. I shared my frustration with them and assured them that we would find a way for them to succeed. I just needed them to remain receptive and not to give up. Success results from finding the best avenue for students to allow them to understand and succeed in class.

NOTES

7 Terministic Screens, Alternative Lessons, and Real Talk Discussions

Teaching students at-promise is typically very challenging. As the pedagogy is slowly but surely implemented, however, students at-promise will reveal themselves as some of the brightest, engaging, and most fulfilling people you will have the privilege to serve. Crucial to this revelation is understanding their terministic screens.

Terministic Screens and Alternative Lessons

Although dialogue is useful and beneficial in gaining glimpses of students' terministic screens, Real Talk is ultimately the key to the most encompassing and insightful understanding of their terministic screens and thereby of their insight and lives. This understanding is crucial to the overall, long-term success in working with students at-promise in the classroom. As discussed earlier, you cannot use Real Talk on a daily basis to increase students' passing rates. When you do use it, keep notes, both mentally and physically, about what you learn from your students to more effectively incorporate their terministic screens.

I used terministic screens in two specific ways. The first was in the continual creation of new and relevant Real Talks throughout the semester. We will discuss Real Talks further later in this chapter. The second was in the creation and implementation of alternative lessons. As defined in Chapters 1 and 2, an alternative lesson is one in which the content standard(s) from the curriculum is combined with the students' terministic screens or with societal issues outside the classroom that connect with students' terministic screens. When we lack students' terministic screens or when we wish to diversify things in the classroom, we must introduce societal issues with which students can connect—issues that students find interesting or that will generate their interest.

Alternative lessons resonate with students, inducing their involvement in the lessons, much more than listening to a teacher deliver a lesson by talking at the class. Alternative lessons connect students to material that typically seems irrelevant, leading them to become more receptive to the material and making the material less threatening or boring. Although these lessons often begin with material seemingly far removed from the curriculum content, the connection to the material the students must learn eventually becomes quite clear. Students typically flesh out their personal connections with the alternative lesson as they understand more clearly how the material connects to their lives at some level.

In my classes, some students shared negative perspectives about specific racial groups based on past experiences or incidents. I used their terministic screens on race relations as a foundation for an alternative lesson. We began with a 10- to 15-minute discussion on their negative experiences with other racial groups. I also shared experiences I had had with other racial groups. Within our discussion, many students shared disturbing experiences and the strong emotions they still felt about them. I extracted a few of the generalizations some of them had made about entire racial groups based on one or two experiences they had had with a specific individual. The students gave examples of situations in which they felt they had been discriminated against. One of these incidents was based on the students' comparison of how an individual had approached them in a department store with how the same individual had approached others in the same location. When the situations were ambiguous, they deduced that they were victims of racial discrimination.

As I highlighted these statements, I transitioned into the curriculum, connecting it to their experiences. I created an alternative lesson using the core concepts of comparing and contrasting, identifying style and tone, making inferences, understanding motivation, and drawing conclusions. We discussed how these concepts were all used within their experiences with racism.[1] They compared and contrasted their treatment in the department store with the treatment of the other people. They compared and contrasted the style and tone the person who approached them used in speaking to them. In the ambiguous situations, the students inferred and drew conclusions regarding racial discrimination against them. I then explained that although I could see what had motivated their dislike for specific groups, they were using an incorrect generalization in assuming that the actions of a few people from a specific group reflect the actions of every person in that group. We then used the GED Steck-Vaughn book (Northcutt et al., 2002) and other resources to review different passages to identify the same concepts. In the final component of the lesson, students read short stories regarding people who had been victims of racial discrimination within the United States and the impact it had had on their lives. Thus, as a result of using students' terministic screens regarding race relations, the students were extremely engaged and willingly did the work to identify and use the concepts taught within the lesson.

One of the most challenging things teachers face in any writing class is getting students to write. Writing is a scary process for students for a multitude of reasons; some of them won't even write their names, let alone an entire sentence. The key for me was to get them to write before we tackled the rules of successful writing. Through Real Talks, I learned that many of my students had developed skills, talents, and tremendous inner strength because of their life experiences. However, they had been overwhelmed with unfair, cruel, and negative critiques from people in positions of power within their lives. Through their terministic screens, the world was a place where they had to hide what they were good at doing. Therefore, I created an alternative lesson that was a writing assignment, based on students' terministic screens, titled "The Me You Don't Know."

As part of the assignment, I asked them to read a one-page paper to understand what I was asking of them. The paper was about an anonymous man who had been belittled, mentally terrorized, and treated like a monster because he did not fit in where he grew up. The young man was extremely shy and lacked confidence. His physical appearance was quite different, even grotesque. However, no one knew his one major strength, not even those closest to him: He was a powerful public speaker who could captivate audiences. Speaking in front of audiences was the only place he felt free. When he was delivering an address, he did not worry about his personal deficiencies, about being considered physically grotesque or different from those around him.

After the students read the paper, I asked them what they thought the young man felt and whether they were surprised about his strength, given how he felt about himself. Many students felt sorry for the guy because he was hurt. Some thought the story was sad because the man only felt free on stage. Others responded that they were very surprised that he could speak in front of audiences in a powerful manner even though he was personally insecure. As the class finished giving their thoughts, I announced, "The Me You Don't Know." At first, students were perplexed as I explained that I was the person in the story.[2] Then they smiled, laughed, and ultimately understood that I was asking them to write about themselves. I was also specifically asking my students to share something that no one—or very few people—knew they could do well. To ensure their comfort level, I had them write anonymously. I also gave them no time restrictions to avoid unneeded pressure as they became more comfortable with writing.

I was pleasantly surprised when many of the students who typically were unwilling to write even one sentence wrote so much during one class period. Some wrote two and three pages to share their version of "The Me You Don't Know." Not only did I get them to write through this alternative lesson, but I also learned a great deal about them through their tremendous papers. My unassuming students were outstanding artists, musicians, athletes, charismatic leaders, and people with tremendous passion. As we progressed, I used their papers to teach them how to transform them into the appropriate writing needed to pass the GED and to succeed overall academically. Their fear of writing dissipated over the course of the semester, and they began to see themselves as capable writers.

Thus, alternative lessons offer unlimited resources for teaching students the necessary material in their classes or standardized tests. They also offer opportunities to challenge their terministic screens. Through the particular lesson I used, I began confronting their terministic screen that teachers are not trustworthy, dismantling their hesitancy or fear in encountering people in authoritative positions.

Real Talk

Real Talk discussions are the most powerful tool in the pedagogy. Through them, you can speak with students on universal themes (e.g., sadness, anger, frustration, happiness, excitement) and tap into their terministic screens, passions, fields of expertise, and experiences to establish powerful connections. With my students, I used Real Talk in diverse ways, ranging from building connections with students to inspiring them, and from helping students focus or regain focus to linking students into curriculum standards they struggled with in class. Real Talk allows teachers to look beyond the superficial shell created in the traditional teacher–student relationship to see the person behind the student. In turn, students can see the person behind the teacher. Thus, we gain insight into each other, which leads to understanding our likes, dislikes, and, most important, our passions.

The expertise, interests, and passions of students will vary, ranging from musical talents such as singing, rapping, or playing an instrument to artistic expressions such as drawing or painting to active endeavors such as boxing, athletics, or customizing cars. One of the objectives in finding students' terministic screens, passions, interests, fields of expertise, strengths, and weaknesses is to pique their investment and involvement in class. As a result of Real Talk, students share the struggles and successes they experience in their everyday lives. This further enriches the classroom and helps educators to understand the reasons students struggle to succeed in school and to find ways to help them succeed despite their everyday struggles.

Structuring Real Talk Discussions

Creating and delivering Real Talks can be exhausting at times because of their personal nature. But every discussion you facilitate will be worthwhile because it has a remarkable impact on the students and their learning. Real Talks give you the most insight into students' terministic screens, which you can use to create new and consistently more relevant Real Talks. I designed the overall structure to integrate and implement Real Talk into classes in an unobtrusive, natural way. Real Talk should never be forced or approached in a manner that makes it seem artificial. Students see through such artificiality and lose their receptiveness and respect for us as teachers. Before the beginning of every semester, I reviewed the curricular standards. I then selected a diverse, broad set of universal themes to use in my classes. In determining these themes, I drew on my personal life experiences or those of friends, loved ones, or people I learned about to create and select my Real Talks. The next set of Real Talks I created was not necessarily directly connected to the curriculum. Instead, these talks were focused more on making overall connections and enhancing relationships with my students in the classroom.

As mentioned previously, I used the first Real Talk strategically on the first day of class to debunk the notion of the teacher as an entity in the classroom. I showed my students that I was a real person willing to reveal parts of myself to connect with them as people rather than as students (see Appendix F). This initial Real Talk established the nontraditional approach I would use to teach and convey my expectations of my students. I exemplified teaching not simply as a job but as my personal connection to education. I used it to show my desire to connect each student to education in a manner best suited to that person instead of forcing my students to learn in the manner imposed on them by so many teachers in their past. Starting the semester in this way typically garnered a powerful, positive response: gaining the respect of my students. Earning their respect was a positive step in building a relationship through which I could effectively teach and students could willingly and openly learn.

Other Real Talks were also implemented strategically throughout the semester. For example, at midsemester, students were typically tired, homesick, and frustrated with school. Keeping them focused on their schoolwork was challenging. However, it was also the perfect time to interject a Real Talk to help them overcome this midsemester lull. However, as I looked for opportunities to use Real Talks appropriately, I understood that overuse could minimize their effectiveness. By placing Real Talks strategically, I kept students wanting more, anticipating the next "special" talk.

I connected some Real Talks directly to the curriculum by tying them into the material students needed to know. Doing so lessened the threatening impact of the curriculum and established student receptiveness to the material. These Real Talks were not alternative lessons. Although the two are somewhat similar, alternative lessons have a far more specific but equally important role within the pedagogy: to connect curriculum content directly with the class. Real Talks have a complementary role to alternative lessons, as does the rest of the pedagogy. Thus, when I tied Real Talks to the curriculum, I placed them strategically where students needed the most help or motivation, typically involving concepts or sections in the curriculum that students usually found difficult (see Appendix E). Through the talks, students found the material more approachable and enjoyable. Students were also more able to relate to the material because the talks were connected to their terministic screens.

As most teachers do, I created some of these Real Talks as part of my preparation for new classes. When creating Real Talks before meeting my students, I focused on universal themes (e.g., happiness, frustration, emptiness, triumph) and connected these themes to myself. My overall objective was to connect with students on a universal and personal level. Even though I did not personally know my students, I could count on them having experienced happiness, anger, frustration, eagerness, fear, hate, and love, regardless of what had caused them to feel these things. The personal component involved sharing various aspects of my personal life. Regardless of who my students were, the personal component was dependent on my own truth and personal testament because I could not depend heavily on my students. Both the universal and the personal components are the beginning parts of all Real Talks structurally and are important tools that I relied on as I first met my students and got to know them. I also had to remain flexible when implementing any of the Real Talks created prior to meeting my students, adjusting or changing things to ensure appropriateness and relevancy for my students.

Based on what I learned about my students from Real Talks, I created additional Real Talks to add to the set. This allowed me to replace Real Talks I'd used previously with new ones based on the insights I'd gained into my students. By creating reusable, adaptable Real Talks, I developed a deep pool from which to draw to match the needs of my students at any given point in the semester.

The final component of structuring Real Talks is learning to trust yourself enough to use Real Talks at a moment's notice, otherwise known as the teachable moment. Rather than letting these moments simply pass by, capture them with Real Talks to enhance and connect with the students' learning experience. Although you may have experienced many teachable moments, you have to learn how to incorporate Real Talks systematically to maximize these opportunities.

When students shared things or certain topics arose that stimulated a Real Talk moment, I realized that I had to take ownership and accept that no one knew my class better than the students and I did. I became comfortable and flexible enough to put aside or modify any lesson or activity to incorporate the ad hoc Real Talk. I looked for opportunities to connect my life experiences to what students were saying to connect everything back to them. Although I did not do this every day, these Real Talks were wonderful supplements to keep us connected throughout the entire semester. After every new spur-of-the-moment creation, I documented the Real Talk for potential future use. Doing so also contributed to the body of knowledge I was building concerning my Real Talk discussions with students. That information served in the creation of additional Real Talks for future classes based on sharing powerful components of actual students' lives with future students. Of course, I always ensured the anonymity of my students in these Real Talks. Names and dates were never included to maintain anonymity.

As with everything within PRT, Real Talk itself has to be flexible to accommodate diverse sets of students. You can incorporate Real Talks for a number of reasons, ranging from connecting with students overall to connecting specifically to concepts or curriculum standards to helping students overcome the obstacles they face throughout the semester. Real Talks allow you to be as encompassing as possible in teaching students. They afforded balance and helped me avoid becoming the overbearing, emotionally draining teacher in the classroom that students disregard.

Preparing Real Talks before meeting my students was crucial to establish the purpose of Real Talk in the classroom. Developing the ability to use Real Talks when there were teachable moments was a powerful component as well. Besides the strategically placed Real Talks (beginning, middle, and close to the end of the semester), the number of Real Talks I used with my classes was best determined from semester to semester as I got to know each set of new students. Although I established dates for using Real Talk, I always remained in tune with my students and receptive to their needs to determine how and when I used Real Talks.

Overall, Real Talks served an important role in class on multiple levels, although I never solely relied on them to teach my students. Implementing these discussions at a moment's notice also took time to master but ultimately strengthened my success as a teacher and my students' success in class. Through Real Talks, both preplanned and spontaneous, I effectively helped my students increase their passing rates.

The Effects of Real Talks

Several students enlightened me about the impact of Real Talk in the classroom. Many students defined their former teachers as "fake" and stressed the importance of teachers who were "real" with them. One student articulated the clearest explanation of a fake teacher:

> First of all, they don't want me in the class, and the way they treat me I can tell they don't like me. Teachers have tried to

talk to me about shit other than school, but they feel sorry for me, judge me, and try to tell me what to do. They don't "feel me," care, or understand my struggles and pains. They were about how they sound and look to others, not about really helping me out. It's about what they gain by trying to help me and I can see right through all that. They never really put themselves out there so I could see who they truly are. Shit, Paul, they focus on supposedly trying to help me, but they always keep their judgmental eyes on me to see how I respond. I am not stupid and neither are the other students, but this is what we have always dealt with, these fake-ass teachers our whole lives.

This student's explanation characterized the opinions that many of my students openly and eagerly shared about teachers. Their perspectives of fake teachers led to their acknowledgement of real teachers. When any of the students in my case study discussed an effective instructor, they used that term: *real*. The realness factor stemmed from our in-class discussions of real-life feelings, emotions, and events.

However, my approach in treating and teaching students was not the only factor that made my class seem real. Students identified the specific, strategically placed lectures fostering open discussions as the thing that made the class seem real. One student described these lectures, which I later termed "Real Talk":

> He [Paul] connects everything in class to real-life stuff that we have all experienced somehow. His class inspires because of the kind of things we talk about. The subjects we talk about are just so inspirational to me and it makes me feel like I can do anything. He is so inspirational to me when he drops his Real Talk on the class.

Another student commented,

> He always talking about that real shit. He tells it like it is and lets us say what we want in the class as well. He does not hide anything from us when doing his Real Talk, and it really opens me up to listening and sharing my real life situations outside of HEP. I wish teachers would have done what Paul does when he does Real Talk in class.

These students' comments highlight that my perspective or experience matching theirs didn't necessarily matter. It was the willingness to "not hide" and to listen to what the students had to say.

Using Real Talk in the classroom helped me tremendously in keeping my students focused, dedicated, inspired, and driven. Such characteristics are rarely representative of students at-promise. One student stated,

> He [Paul] really breaks things down so I understand them. He gives examples straight from his life and our lives (students) as well. Like not exact experiences from our lives but shit that we can relate to in life. Like he talks about the struggles in life, being broke, working hard and not getting nowhere, experiencing racism, and just all kinds of shit. Every time it's different. I mean, I can really connect with that stuff. It keeps me interested in what is going on in class because you never know when that real stuff is coming.

Real Talk created genuine interest in the class that helped maintain students' attention and focus on what they were supposed to learn. I integrated multiple Real Talks throughout the semester to keep students alert and constantly to include their thoughts, feelings, and emotions in our class culture. The students expressed looking forward to the Real Talk discussions, which made them an integral part of the class:

> He just is on some real shit. He really teaches us about life, how to get ready for the future and what's on the GED. It's strange because he combines everything so well in our classes. I love it when he gets in front of the class and he leads our special talks. He digs deep and gets us all sayin' some of the deepest shit I have ever heard in a class. I mean he is right about shit when he talks about us having to deal with shit in the past and in the future but he keeps us motivated and ready to pass his classes. Our talks are a part of what makes the class so real to me and why I love going to class.

With some Real Talk discussions, I tied the conversations back to the core concepts by reintroducing them within the discussion. For example, when one student led a Real Talk on pain, I connected it to the concepts of summarizing major ideas and analyzing tone. I did this by asking students to summarize how the student leader felt based on her tone of voice and the main ideas of her story. After students shared their thoughts, we transitioned to the lesson in the book that dealt with the concepts. One young man explained,

> Paul [is] always making class fun and interesting. Everything about class is like real life. It ain't no boring ass teacher shit, but some stuff that we can use when we go back home. I never been in a class that I really understood until I came into this class. He be making it all easy for us and I be talking in that class because I want to learn more. I ask questions and tell everybody what I think because he don't hate on me. I feel like I am part of the class, like I help by being involved and it helps me because I get my questions answered.

This particular student's enthusiasm in the class was only matched by his dedication to learning and passing the standardized test. Another student said,

> He is just real. He don't judge me and works real hard for me and the class. He inspires me because I feel like I can do anything in his class and out in the world. . . . It is just a lot of fun to be in his class. Learning things in his class is so easy because it is all about real life and we just be doing work in there like it is easy. Paul really cares about us and he pushes us to be the best so we can pass the GED. My confidence really has gone up because he keeps showing me that I really am smart and not dumb like teachers have always made me feel.

As the semester progressed, Real Talk stimulated students to share their thoughts and open up to the entire class. Students began taking initiative in class through leading the Real Talks. As they shared their experiences and connected them to the class, they inspired other students. I always tried to integrate these student-led discussions with the remainder of the class. I allowed and encouraged students to share their insights, which created a powerful, positive environment in the class. Thus, students took ownership of the Real Talk sessions.

Eventually, a physical impact of Real Talk in the classroom was apparent. When students thought or felt I was going to begin a Real Talk, they sat at the edge of their seats in anticipation of delving into our powerful talks. The students, like so many other students at-promise, seldom remained quiet during class when a teacher was speaking, but

Real Talk activated the "pin-drop phenomenon": The students became so engaged and captivated that one could literally hear a pin drop in our classroom. For students who seldom dedicated their full attention to a teacher in the classroom to become so engaged gave tremendous insight into the effects of Real Talk with students.

Another interesting phenomenon accredited to Real Talk involved students who tested out of my classes. Only a handful of students occasionally qualified to test out of some of their classes. These students were typically more advanced academically compared with the majority of the students in the program. For example, some students who were very strong in reading might be struggling in the other four GED subjects (science, writing, math, and social studies). We allowed them to take the reading exam for the GED early so they could focus on their weaker subjects and have one less exam to stress about. The instructors and associate director determined which students qualified, based on their practice test scores, quizzes, and overall work. Students who tested out of a subject were no longer permitted to attend sessions for that class but were required to attend the classes of the subjects still needed.

What I encountered in my reading and writing classes with the students who tested out was both exceptional and humbling to experience as their teacher: Many of my students asked if they could continue to attend my class. They wanted to be a part of the lectures and learning we had created using this pedagogy. Most frequently, students identified Real Talk as the major reason they wanted to remain in my class. They shared that these special talks and the connections they felt in class were something they wanted to maintain—that those things helped them stay focused, motivated, inspired, and driven to do their overall work within the program. Having a student at-promise who no longer needed or was permitted to attend a class but asked to continue to attend was almost unheard of not only within the program but also in any other academic setting.

Thus, what Real Talk was intended to do was clearly taking place and having an immense impact on the students. Although their test scores ultimately needed to reflect the impact of the pedagogy (as it clearly did in the study), it was equally important for me to have the perspective of the students. Students shared that our classroom was a safe haven, a place where they belonged instead of where they were treated like a burden in society. The students determined what was effective for them in the classroom, and their insight was of the utmost importance to me not only as a researcher but also especially as a teacher. The credentials I held that allowed me to stand before them and teach did not give me the insight to determine what they felt was best for them. Only with their help could I determine what suited them best in learning in my class.

Real Talk and alternative lessons are a breakthrough in establishing connections, generating interest in the subject matter, and providing an arena for students to learn material they normally resisted. As you learn more about your students, you must continue the sequence of adaptation and involvement of student experiences in the required content. You must continue creating powerful, relevant Real Talks and alternative lessons to captivate students and spark their interest in learning based on the information gleaned from Real Talks, students' terministic screens, and their personal experiences.

Thus, a group of students who were at one time considered apathetic, hostile, and cynical toward education will flourish and embrace the education process as they prepare to pass their classes and best prepare for standardized exams. No longer will they merely be going through the motions of attending class. They will be engaged and willingly share their understanding of the world. Thus, through their voices, the success of PRT is solidified.

Notes

1. The title of this lesson was "Have You Ever Been a Victim of Racism? How Do You Know You Have Experienced Racial Discrimination?"
2. If teachers are not comfortable using themselves in this lesson, they may choose someone else.

Implementing Real Talk in Any Classroom 8

We've discussed what PRT is and how it was implemented in a variety of classrooms. Ultimately, PRT can be translated successfully into any classroom, providing educators are willing to make the changes and connections necessary to engage their students in the process. In fact, since the creation of PRT, it has been adopted and used by hundreds of educators around the country, and results show that it can be used successfully by anyone who is willing to earnestly try and implement this pedagogical approach.

I have had the privilege of working with K–12 institutions, universities, community colleges, and educational nonprofit organizations around the world to train them in my approach. The pedagogy is not limited to any one type of institution; it can work within diverse settings where professionals want to enhance success with students. The applicability of the approach has ranged from administrators in universities seeking ways to teach their student-support staff how to connect with students at-promise; centers for teaching and learning in community colleges trying to develop their faculties' teaching in the classroom; and nonprofit organizations that wanted to infuse engaging pedagogy in their programming. In diverse educational settings, the pedagogy has proven to be useful and effective.

In the following sections, I have provided more in-depth detail on how educators can be trained, the basic components of the pedagogy, establishing connections, Real Talk and alternative lessons, and the applicability of the training. The reason this approach was created is to ensure its usability by others so they could find success with their students. Additionally, this approach ensures that others can also maintain that success over time with as many students as possible.

Therefore, the purpose of this chapter is to help educators understand how to apply PRT in their classrooms. I am hopeful that educators will incorporate the approach in its entirety—or at least components of it—to transform their teaching and become more successful in their chosen craft.

Educators must keep in mind that the only way we will continue to serve our students best is through continual professional growth. We must avoid the pitfall of becoming complacent with our teaching strategies. We must challenge ourselves to learn new things that we can feasibly apply in the classroom that will make an impact on our students, especially our students at-promise. Through PRT, we can actively seek to connect with our students and learn from them. We can then combine what we learn with the material we must teach.

Ms. D is a teacher who embraces a commitment to growth and rejects complacency. After 10 years as a high school teacher, Ms. D was frustrated by her lack of success with students at-promise and was willing to learn PRT. Ms. D was already a very good teacher when I first met her, yet she felt that there was room for growth in her approach to teaching. This set the tone for our work together. She was trained for an academic year, implementing the various strategies as she learned them. Each year, the district statistician analyzed student passing rates by teacher. Her student passing rate after her implementation of the pedagogy was 8.8 percent greater than her previous year's passing rate (Hernandez, 2011, p. 2).

Although I could easily apply my pedagogy in the classroom and explain it to others, I found that training someone else to use it consistently and effectively in the classroom was more challenging. One extremely valuable lesson I learned from Ms. D was that my approach only worked with those willing to try it wholeheartedly, agreeing to push themselves out of their comfort zones while striving to improve their teaching in the classroom. Ms. D exemplified these traits. Her focus was never on herself but on her students; she was constantly willing to learn and grow to better serve her students at-promise. Her willingness to implement the plans I helped her create was instrumental in helping me become more efficient and proficient in sharing this pedagogy.

Training others with the pedagogy on a broader scale occurred organically. While training Ms. D, I presented at several conferences, sharing the foundations of the pedagogy, my initial study, and the progress Ms. D and I were making with her students. At these conferences, teachers, professors, and administrators inquired more and more about the pedagogy and opportunities for training. Realizing the opportunity to help educators, I selected a few of the schools as pilot sites for training in the pedagogy. As a result, I have provided training in a wide array of settings and with diverse groups of teachers and professors. In every case, the schools and educators I worked with were self-selected; they were not required to participate in my training.

The teachers and professors in my training sessions have come from a wide range of schools: traditional and alternative, rural and urban. They have also been extremely diverse demographically: men and women, different racial groups and ages, new and veteran teachers, and with varied levels of skill. Some teachers were extremely successful with the students in their classrooms; some faced great struggles in working with students at-promise. What they all had in common, however, was a willingness to try something new and to move out of their comfort zone. They all selflessly admitted that they had room to grow as educators in the classroom.

Although each classroom situation is different and every class of students is unique, the practicality and beauty of this pedagogical model is that educators can adapt it to meet the diverse needs of any group of students in any subject area. All that is needed is the willingness of the educator to connect and to adapt and to believe that the students want to succeed, even when they don't know how to do so and seemingly sabotage their own efforts at every turn. Instructors of any subject can genuinely care for their students' success, relate to their students while viewing and treating them as equals, and dedicate time to understanding their students. We are the professionals. It is our task to meet our students' needs and to help them succeed. PRT can serve as another tool to help us achieve these goals.

PART II: IMPLEMENTATION

PART III

Taking PRT to Scale

Chapter 9: Professional Development — 114

Chapter 10: Professional Development: Alternative Lessons — 132

Chapter 11: New Beginnings — 145

9 Professional Development

The first section of this chapter is to suggest a potential structure or outline that educators can use when training others in PRT. Ultimately, it is up to the facilitator to decide how to do this, but I have found the PRT Institute (noted earlier) is a structure that works well with teachers when scaling and sustaining the approach within a school. The PRT Institute's strength is the intensive training model focused on helping teachers become competent with PRT methods for connecting and engaging with students at-promise, as opposed to a conference or short-term training approach. As I mentioned in Chapter 4, PRT is relevant for students at-promise and all students' success. The PRT Teacher Institute's outcomes help institutions improve student success and increase retention, persistence, and completion. During the PRT Institute, teachers learn, create, practice, and implement PRT in their classrooms.

After several years of "one-and-done"–type professional development, either as a participant or facilitator, I realized participants need more time to develop and implement new skills. Of course, one-day professional development has value and is important, but it does not support the consistent large-scale transformational approach needed. Research supports that inconsistent professional development does not help most teachers effectively develop and implement new classroom skills (Truesdale, 2009). Thus, teachers need the support and commitment from schools to develop the additional skills necessary to transform their classrooms. Too often, initiatives to improve student success come and go with few changes or improvements, especially within classrooms. It's important to note that successfully institutionalizing PRT at any school requires a long-term commitment.

Using the PRT Institute training structure creates what Malcolm-Piqueux and Bensimon (2020) refer to as developing best practitioners—developing teachers further to serve their students better. Every school, teacher, and student is unique. Within this professional development model, teachers apply the work through their own unique experiences and then combines it with what they learn from their students. Teachers take what they learn and make it a part of their everyday teaching in the classroom. Through this approach, teachers will become best practitioners. The training framework is scalable, sustainable, and evolves over time. Rather than discuss the entire structure of the PRT Institute, I will share a condensed version of the first year's training design for facilitators beginning this work to use as a guide.

The first step in creating a PRT Institute at your institution is to select the participating teachers. The selection process can take many forms, including a formal application process, appointing interested participants, or having teachers opt-in to a broad call for participation. It is essential in this process that the training opportunity is optional. You must also plan for and expect a percentage of teachers who will choose not to participate. I have learned over the years that most teachers who choose not to attend are simply not interested. Working with a person or group of people who are forced to do something against their will is extremely complicated. They are uncooperative, unreceptive, resistant, and negative, and they often disengage from the group. By making participation in the training voluntary, you separate out the teachers who are not interested. However, because teaching is a highly personal craft, do not be offended when teachers are uninterested.

Training days typically occur over summer months when most teacher's schedules are more flexible. The training consists of four, six-hour days. All participants should read PRT before the training days. Although I am sharing concepts to use in training, I am leaving facilitators room to add relevant content to complete the training agendas for their training's purpose. A variety of breaks, including a lunch break, should be incorporated into each day's schedule. The order of break periods is at the discretion of the facilitator.

During the training, teachers learn about, create, and practice Real Talks and alternative lessons, amongst other concepts discussed in Chapter 3. Throughout the four training days, teachers are active learners—listening; asking questions; working individually, in small groups, or as an entire group; and creating content. The training space you want to create is transparent, safe, judgment-free, and allows people to be curious. Embracing diverse perspectives and varying levels of understanding from each participant must be possible. The facilitator's approach should be to lift people up instead of tearing them down by guiding each person with positivity and constructive criticism.

Start with a beginner's mind on Day 1. I often encounter teachers who rightfully consider themselves experts in their teaching or subject matter but fail to recognize Suzuki and Dixson's (2006) observation about intellectual growth: "The mind of the beginner is empty, free of the habits of the expert, ready to accept, to doubt and open to all possibilities" (p. xiv). Transforming teaching requires participants to continually revise what they think they already know. When participants start with a beginner's mind, it's possible for participant groups to be open-minded and move forward with curiosity. This atmosphere encourages creativity among the group as they develop new skills.

Introducing vulnerability—how it is defined and why it matters for this work—takes place next as part of the first day of training. I use Dr. Brené Brown's (2010) TEDx Talk "The Power of Vulnerability" to introduce vulnerability. After showing the video, begin either large- or small-group discussions about participants' thoughts on what they heard and why it matters. As the discussions conclude, it is important to bring the group back to the specific purpose of vulnerability in the classroom. To conduct Real Talk means teachers must be willing to be vulnerable with students in the classroom. This exploration leads to the next topic, "Why is Real Talk important?" The facilitator can convey this content through a presentation and ask participants questions to expand their understanding of why it is important. The point here is to help participants understand Real Talk's power and effectiveness in the classroom and the impact on student success. Additionally, when participants can ask questions, the facilitator can clarify misconceptions or confusion.

Now the facilitator must carefully define Real Talk, which is the most important part of the first day. Explaining Real Talk is best done using other teachers' and the facilitator's Real Talk case studies to deepen the understanding of Real Talk. When I explain Real Talk, I use six different examples from teachers in various subject matters and with different universal themes. The examples shared can vary in format, from written Real Talks to recorded Real Talks, or you can share examples of Real Talks you have observed. Real Talk can be brought to life when the facilitator shares her or his own during the training. There will undoubtedly be questions, but the facilitator should encourage the group to ask more questions to ensure complete clarity about what an effective Real Talk is.

The remainder of Day 1 is spent with the group creating original Real Talks. I dedicate an hour and a half for participants to create their Real Talks, with instructions to reconvene after time expires. Participants must be encouraged to work however they feel most comfortable. For example, some people may want to work alone while others may want to work in small groups. Also, participants should be allowed to work from wherever they like. If the professional development is held at the school, some people will choose to go to their classroom, office, or somewhere else within the facility. The point is for people to feel comfortable so they can be authentic as they create their Real Talks. During the work time, the facilitator must be available to participants and ready to answer questions or discuss whatever participants have in mind regarding their Real Talks. Once the allotted time ends and the group is back together, the facilitator ends the day with two announcements. First, remind the group they should continue working on their Real Talks in the evening and be prepared to share with the group the following day. Second, revisit the day and ask the group if they have any questions before concluding.

Day 2 begins with a focus on creating a sense of belonging for students in the classroom, which can take the form of large- or small-group activities, watching an inspirational video followed by discussion prompts, or discussion prompts for large- or small-group dialogue. Ensuring people understand what a sense of belonging means and looks like in the classroom is the intended outcome. Once the group understands sense of belonging, introduce the group to the day's feedback protocol. To set the parameters and tone the group will use to interact through the day of Real Talks, instruct participants to thoughtfully consider the Real Talks they observe with the following framework: What did you see, hear, and wonder during your colleagues' Real Talks? Before sharing Real Talks, allow participants a final opportunity to refine their Real Talks through a pair-and-share process. Pair and share eases participants into sharing their Real Talks while creating an opportunity for feedback before sharing with the entire group. As is the case for many teachers, participants will find it more challenging to deliver Real Talks to colleagues than their students. This reservation is normal and part of the experience. Once the pair and shares conclude, sharing Real Talks with the entire group begins.

The number of participants you have will determine how much of the day is spent sharing Real Talks and receiving feedback. Most commonly, sharing and feedback consume the rest of the day. It is critical for all participants to share their Real Talk, but they gain the most value in hearing feedback from colleagues and the facilitator. Additionally, ask all participants to describe the experience of creating a Real Talk, how it felt to deliver the Real Talk in front of the group, and what was most surprising about creating and delivering a Real Talk. Once the entire process has been completed and they all have shared their Real Talk, the opportunity to remind the group how to appropriately and strategically apply Real Talks comes next.

Reminding the group to select strategic dates to deliver Real Talks is vital. The first day of class, the middle of the semester, and before the end of the semester are three effective times to deliver Real Talks. Some participants may feel uncomfortable with the dates proposed, but remember that this is a guide and not a rule. Ultimately, what matters most is the Real Talks are appropriately conducted in class; timing plays a role, but the teacher's comfort level does too. Once you discuss the strategic placement of Real Talks, provide an opportunity for closing comments or questions. Before closing training for the day, ask participants to bring a laptop to the next training session. Participants will need computers to create alternative lessons, and you should provide a laptop to any participant who needs one. Day 2 is a taxing day for everyone involved, yet two days of professional development remain.

You will notice that the third- and fourth-day structures are similar to the first- and second-day structures. However, Days 3 and 4 cover different topics. The focus of Day 3 should begin with creativity. I use Dr. Ken Robinson's (2006) famous TED Talk "Do Schools Kill Creativity?" but there are many other options to choose from to convey the importance of creativity. After showing the video, begin either large- or small-group discussions surrounding participants' thoughts on what they heard and why it matters. As the discussions conclude, it is important to bring the group back to our work's specific purpose with creativity; to create alternative lessons means they must be willing to take risks by being creative. To introduce why alternative lessons matter, you can again present information and then ask participants questions to expand their understanding of why creativity is important. The point is to help participants understand why alternative lessons are effective and how they impact student success while encouraging participants to ask questions.

Now the facilitator must patiently define alternative lessons. To progress with the training, participants must understand and feel comfortable with alternative lessons. Sharing examples of alternative lessons from other teachers and the facilitator will deepen participants' understanding and highlight the diversity of what alternative lessons can look like. The examples shared should be from different subjects to highlight alternative lessons' flexibility and utility for any subject matter. As I explained with Real Talk, I share at least six different alternative lesson examples with the group. The alternative examples you share can be written, presentations, recordings, or you can share examples based on your experience or observation. Again, one example should be created by the facilitator. Take time to answer questions and encourage the group to ask more questions to achieve a level of clarity that everyone is comfortable with.

For the remainder of the third day, the next step is for the group to create their own alternative lessons. I dedicate an hour and a half for participants to create alternative lessons, and I ask everyone to reconvene once the time is up. Remind participants to use their laptops to access information or resources while creating alternative lessons. Be supportive of people who want to work alone and others who may want to work in small groups. As mentioned before, encourage people to work where they feel most comfortable as they create their alternative lessons. Again, the facilitator must be available to participants and ready to answer questions or discuss whatever participants have in mind regarding their alternative lessons. As with Day 1, once the allotted time ends and the group is back together, the facilitator ends the day with two announcements. First, remind the group they should continue working on their alternative lessons in the evening and be prepared to share with the group the following day. Second, revisit the day and ask the group if they have any questions before concluding. The fourth and final day of training will be an invigorating yet intensive day.

Begin the final day with growth mindset. I use Dr. Carol Dweck's (2014) TED Talk "The Power of Believing That You Can Improve" to introduce growth mindset. As I discussed in Chapter 3, PRT focuses on the teacher's growth mindset. Beginning the day with growth mindset plays an important role in helping participants face the challenging but possible process of transforming their curriculum through alternative lessons. Developing alternative lessons relies on growth mindset, and this focus helps set the tone to support and encourage teachers as they develop and deliver alternative lessons. Remind the group of the feedback protocol for observing and responding to colleagues' alternative lessons, with one addition: What did you see, what did you hear, what did you wonder, and did you understand the concept taught through the alternative lesson? I typically do not encourage pair and share at this point because this process is longer with alternative lessons than Real Talks. Thus, the group begins with their alternative lessons as if they were teaching their class.

Typically, the sharing and feedback of alternative lessons occupies the rest of the day. The feedback process is crucial to the experience, but as mentioned with Real Talk, so is the experience of the presenter. Ask each person these questions: What was your experience with creating an alternative lesson, how did you feel presenting the lesson to the group, and what surprised you the most about creating an alternative lesson? Unlike Real Talks, teachers can use the alternative lessons method every day to transform their curriculum. It's important to remind participants they can continue to create more alternative lessons and use them at will. Comfort and ability to create and deliver alternative lessons will take time and happens at each teacher's unique pace. When everyone's alternative lesson presentations are complete, feedback has been given and received, and questions have been asked and answered, it is time to conclude the day.

The conclusion of the fourth and final day is about reflection and setting expectations for the academic year. Creating a set of questions, either verbally or through a survey, for the group to share their experiences is important. Creating a space for sharing experiences can bring the group closer together and for the facilitator to learn what was effective, what needs improvement, and what the week meant to the individual group members. The next step is for the participants to identify how many Real Talks and alternative lessons they will create and implement during the academic year. This decision is made by the group, and the selected amount can vary. The most common combination is four Real Talks and six alternative lessons for the academic year. With goals set for the year, it is essential to end the intensive and rewarding four days on a positive note. It is up to the facilitator to determine how the day ends specifically, but it's important to bear in mind the participants worked hard; showing respect, appreciation, and support is important for everyone.

The structure I have shared is a good starting point for professional development, paving a path for implementation during the academic year. Remember, this is about teacher development, and developing best practitioners takes time and effort. It also means administrators creating the appropriate budget to compensate teachers participating in the PRT Institute. Ultimately, relationships matter to students, and one of the most essential places students develop relationships is in the classroom. This work is about training teachers how to create and sustain profound relationships in the classroom. Additionally, the design and implementation of the curriculum will determine students' success. This approach develops an inclusive, engaging curriculum that is relevant to students. In turn, by transforming the curriculum, student success will increase. To add clarity with Real Talk and alternative lessons, the remaining section of this chapter provides detailed examples and information about Real Talk, and Chapter 10 focuses more deeply on alternative lessons.

Connections Through Real Talk

As mentioned earlier, it is important to define "Real Talk" and provide examples of Real Talk discussions. Real Talk can be used in many different ways to improve the teaching and learning process. Its purpose is to establish connections, understanding, trust, empathy, and caring for one another between and among teachers and students in the classroom. Through Real Talk, teachers can also gain insight into students' terministic screens. This allows teachers to use Real Talk flexibly in their classrooms based on what they learn from their students. Ultimately, if we cannot establish connections with our students at-promise, our lessons and whatever we are trying to teach them will fail, which, in turn, leads to our students being more resistant to the learning process.

Establishing Real Talk is essential during the first week of a course or class to begin building rapport and connections with students. With more experience, teachers may even integrate Real Talk discussions on the first day of class. Although these discussions are dependent on the students for their direct insight, teachers must initiate the steps in sharing to establish Real Talk in the classroom. One specific way to use Real Talk to build connections is to dismantle the negative stereotypes students may have of teachers because of their past experiences. Through Real Talk, teachers can more comfortably show the person they are behind the position of teacher. Revealing appropriate personal information about ourselves through Real Talks is preferable to students assuming they have no connection to us. By focusing Real Talks on universal themes (e.g., eagerness, happiness, frustration, motivation), teachers can overcome barriers and establish the similarities they share with their students as people. Through such Real Talks, teachers begin to establish powerful connections with their students as the students begin to see the teachers in front of them as persons rather than as generic teachers.

Teachers can also use Real Talks when students' morale is down, when students are not engaged or are frustrated, or to address anything that is inhibiting their students from focusing on the work they must complete in class. However, teachers must remember that Real Talk should not be used on a daily basis. Instead, teachers should incorporate Real Talks systematically yet genuinely in working with their students. As teachers master the use of Real Talk, they must use their discretion concerning how to best use this component in their classrooms.

Real Talks can also be used to help students connect to the material in the curriculum. In all subjects, teachers find particular chapters, concepts, or materials that are exceptionally difficult to teach because they do not generate student interest. Using Real Talk to introduce particularly challenging material often generates student eagerness or willingness to learn the material. Combined with alternative lessons, which we discuss in Chapter 10, Real Talk can increase students' receptivity to the material.

In developing Real Talk sessions, teachers must select themes that they can personalize from life experience to connect with students. The focus is not the exact experiences instructors share but the students' relationship to these universal themes. Using both positive and negative experiences creates broader connections with students, even when no direct similarities exist between the experiences of the students and those of their teachers. The entire process is based on a systematic approach to establish, strengthen, and solidify connections between teachers and students. Teachers can consistently use the understanding and relationships Real Talk generates to connect students to the material they must learn. Thus, teachers elevate students' genuine interest, engagement in class, and motivation to learn.

The following process gives teachers a starting point for creating a Real Talk. Each talk has a beginning, a middle, and an end. Teachers must use explicit transitions to guide and deliver these discussions. Creating a Real Talk requires seven steps, although the steps may vary from person to person. Thus, teachers should use these steps as a guide to begin a Real Talk and determine which steps are most useful to them:

1. Choose a theme and create your Real Talk outside of class.

2. Adjust your demeanor when delivering the Real Talk to captivate students; begin with a leading question.

3. Begin your Real Talk broadly, define the universal theme, and then share your Real Talk.

4. Ask students if they have experienced this theme.

5. Ask students to share their examples of dealing with the theme.

6. Build connections between the various examples the students have shared.

7. End the Real Talk in one of two ways: Connect the Real Talk to what you are teaching that day or simply conclude the Real Talk with what you have shared.

Although this step-by-step breakdown of Real Talk may seem tedious or long-winded, in reality the process flows naturally, concisely, and rhythmically.

Step 1

Before any Real Talk is delivered with students, it must first be created outside of the class. As teachers become more experienced with Real Talks, they can create them instantaneously in class. First, teachers select a universal theme; within that theme, they must determine how they will share their particular experience or story with their students (see Appendix G). When first beginning to use Real Talk, teachers will expend both time and effort in the process. The story or experience exemplifying the chosen theme must make sense. The teacher must also be very careful not to use vernacular that is specific to the teacher but to use language that is easily understood by the students. Very often, teachers write out their Real Talks for review. I consistently find that, given their education, they write and want to deliver a Real Talk based on language that is easily understood by a college-educated audience. The problem is that our students do not necessarily use or understand the same language or the meanings of words in the same way as the teacher. Thus, many things that make sense to the teachers need to be described in a different manner for their students.

Once the Real Talks are written out, teachers need to practice them before conducting the actual Real Talks in their classrooms. Practice is not intended to create a formal presentation or an over-rehearsed delivery of a speech. Instead, it is to help teachers feel comfortable and to be succinct and purposeful (while maintaining authenticity) with the delivery of a Real Talk. Too often, we witness people with powerful messages or meaningful things to share but with weak or seemingly scattered delivery. This makes it difficult for the intended audience to follow the message and causes the audience to disengage from what is being said. Practicing allows teachers to trust themselves and to resist deviating from their intended purpose in delivering a Real Talk. However, I must stress that this practice is not about preparing a keynote speech, workshop or class presentation, or formal speech. Here, practice allows teachers to identify areas for improvement to enhance the quality of their Real Talks further in the hope of building connectedness with their students.

Step 2

Delivering the Real Talk in the classroom begins with the teacher changing his or her demeanor and the selection of the questions that the teacher will ask surrounding the identified universal theme. By *change demeanor*, I mean teachers must purposely change the manner in which they stand in front of the class, their tone of voice, the extent to which they show emotion, and any other physical and verbal actions they commonly use when working with their students. Teachers must be very specific and evident as they immediately prepare to ask their students their leading question. The teacher's demeanor should be one of mixed emotions. For example, the teacher's voice should have a slightly more serious tone without being authoritative, a tone showing the teacher is both earnest and vulnerable. However, within that vulnerability, teachers must remain in control of emotions. Too much emotion will disconnect the students from what the teacher is trying to relay. This change in demeanor will also help students sense that their teachers are going to deliver something different from the usual lecture or discussion.

On changing demeanor, the teacher's first interaction using Real Talk with students is to ask a question embedded with the universal theme. This is the initial hook when beginning a Real Talk. For example, a teacher asked her students, "Does anyone know what rejection means?" Or another example: "Has anyone in class ever felt angry because they were so frustrated?" The question is not one that is necessarily meant to be answered; rather, it is more rhetorical in nature. Although teachers will notice that the question will grab the attention of the students as it is meant to, they should not wait for students to answer the question literally. Its purpose is to attract their attention. Teachers may hear some students make comments in agreement with the question or physically show their agreement. Once teachers have asked the question and have their students' attention, teachers should immediately delve into the Real Talk.

Worth noting is that as you progress and improve on your usage of Real Talk, it will not always be necessary to pose a question to your students. For example, as you improve, you can start by making a statement, followed by your personal experience or whatever you decide to share with your students. Another method is to use visuals of something that is personal to you and begin to share your experience surrounding the image you are showing. Regardless of how you begin, you should always hook students. You should also keep a universal theme within all Real Talks, whether explicit or implicit. The more you do Real Talk, the more comfortable and better you will get at using it and making the necessary adjustments that best fit your needs.

Step 3

The teacher begins by talking about what his or her chosen universal theme (e.g., adversity, gratefulness, frustration) means in general, providing a clear definition for students. By beginning broadly, the instructor can funnel the talk into a more detailed, meaningful discussion about a direct experience that begins to connect students to the theme. The first connection occurs when the teacher shares a personal experience with the theme. It is optimal and preferable for teachers to share their own authentic experiences. However, teachers can authentically apply or share the experiences of others with whom they are close, such as friends and family, or use biographies, events, or experiences based on popular culture or media. The point of the teacher sharing these experiences is to deepen the connection between understanding the theme and the reality of experiencing the theme. This also allows the students to see teachers as persons beyond their positions in the classroom.

Step 4

Teachers should then ask the students if they have experienced or know someone who has experienced the theme. By asking if they know someone who has experienced the theme, it allows students who are not comfortable sharing about themselves an opportunity to contribute comfortably. The wording of this request should be an explicit transition from teacher to students. It is not essential that students confirm their experiences with the theme by raising their hands. Any form of agreement (e.g., verbal comments, physically nodding their heads, attentive or positive changes in the atmosphere) is sufficient to acknowledge the students' involvement. When teachers first begin using Real Talk, they may not receive overwhelming response from their classes. This is often because the students are surprised by what their teachers are doing; they are not accustomed to teachers engaging them and sharing in this manner. Teachers will normally notice changes in the demeanor of their classes as the students listen to the Real Talk. Slowly but surely, some students will acknowledge what their teachers are sharing; others may talk with their teachers after class to share the impact of the Real Talk in private. A clear indicator that students are focused on the Real Talk is the pin-drop phenomenon: having a classroom filled with students at-promise so intensely focused on every word their teacher is saying that one can hear a pin drop. The time between asking the question and observing students' responses should be very short. Teachers should also follow this step immediately with Step 5.

Step 5

Teachers should ask students to share any specific examples of dealing with the theme. The sharing can be their own personal examples or examples of someone they know. This should be a strictly voluntary activity. In the first Real Talk in a class, few students will volunteer, although typically at least two or three students offer specific examples. As students share, teachers should be active listeners, remaining reassuring and receptive while listening intently to every word their students are saying. Teachers may also need to help students verbalize their thoughts. Many students are not used to sharing their personal thoughts and may struggle to communicate them verbally. Teachers should help them clarify their explanations and encourage them to help them feel more comfortable.

As students share, the other students commonly listen intently. The atmosphere of the classroom begins to shift as the people within it begin to relate to each other rather than remain a group of disconnected individuals. After each student who wishes to do so shares experiences or insights, teachers should reiterate the connection of those experiences to the theme. Then, proceed to Step 6.

In the event that students do not share, teachers should not assume that the Real Talk was a failure. Teachers must remember to pay close attention to their students throughout the Real Talk. If the students are captivated, completely focused, or engaged with the teacher, that means that the Real Talk is affecting the students. If they do not respond, teachers should proceed to Step 7 to conclude the Real Talk.

Step 6

Teachers should build connections between what the students have shared. Using universal themes, teachers can begin to dismantle differences and highlight similarities. To do this, teachers must show the variations of the theme nearly all people experience and how each student who shared brought one of those variations to light. This method helps students feel empowered in the class, showing them that they are contributing to the overall experience and knowledge of the class.

By helping the class begin to feel empowered, teachers also highlight the commonalities they share through their diverse experiences, which begins to establish the classroom as a safe place to be open and accepting of one another. This step can also affect attendance positively, solidifying the classroom as a place where students feel stability and the freedom to be themselves. Real Talk can transform the classroom into a place where the turmoil many students at-promise typically face within their lives is absent. They do not have to worry about the many things within their lives that add stress, albeit perhaps only for the hour they spend in class.

Step 7

The final step is another transition that concludes the Real Talk. Once teachers garner insight from their students and their experiences, they must connect the Real Talk to what they are teaching in class. If that is not possible, or if the original intent of the Real Talk is not specific to the curriculum, teachers should connect the Real Talk with their students. Teachers may also attempt to do both. For example, in the Real Talk described in Appendix G, the teacher connects adversity to both establishing connections with others and to the curriculum. The teacher shows the students that by passing the class, they are overcoming a form of adversity that the class poses for some students. The students recognize adversity within their own lives and eventually understand that the challenge the curriculum represents for them is a form of adversity that they are facing within their lives. For a plethora of reasons (e.g., lack of effort, lack of understanding, intimidation, personal or family responsibilities), achieving success in school is a big challenge for this population of students, a form of adversity for many of them. Through Real Talk, the teacher identifies that all people share the experience of some form of adversity and, as a result, attempts to bring the class together. Through this Real Talk, the teacher helps students turn the curriculum from an oppositional force that will "beat them" into an obstacle they can overcome by successfully preparing through the work they do in class. Ultimately, the teacher and students work together toward a common goal instead of working against one another in the classroom. Lastly, end every Real Talk on some sort of positive note and not on a negative one.

Another Real Talk Example

As we have discussed previously, giving students a voice in class by incorporating their perspectives and experiences is very important in engaging them with the learning process. More important is the teacher's ability to connect with students and to help connect students' perspectives to the academic curriculum to ensure they meet the final academic goals for the course. As teachers discover the students' terministic screens, they must create or adjust Real Talks and lessons based on this information. In doing so, however, teachers must maintain the integrity of the material, not "water it down." The following paragraphs show an example of a media arts teacher who implemented Real Talk in her classroom.

Giving students a voice in class by incorporating their perspectives and experiences is necessary to engage them with the learning process. More important is the teacher's ability to connect with students and help connect students' perspectives to the academic curriculum so that they meet the course's academic goals. The connections you develop with students are the beginning of creating these vital relationships. In this section, I provide an example from a teacher who used Real Talk to connect with her students.

SP is an energetic, creative teacher committed to her students' success. When we first met, it was evident that she was a constant learner seeking ways to grow as a teacher in the classroom. She knew from her own experience as a student that students need to know that they matter, are capable, and are cared about. She also knew students needed to have space to express knowledge in ways that align with varied learning styles. This perspective gave SP a strong ability to relate to students, but she understood there were ways to further improve. With this in mind, she joined the PRT Institute at her school. What she learned at the PRT Institute complemented her already strong skill set and gave her new insights. She realized Real Talk gave her a structure and intentionality she lacked to more effectively connect with students. It took patience and persistence for SP to implement and experience the power of Real Talk.

SP described the various Real Talks she delivered for her class; the most impactful one was at the end of the semester. She created a Real Talk with a universal theme of individuality. More specifically, she tied it to the individuality in learning (see Appendix H). From her own experience as a learner, SP knew formalized assessments are not always the best way to determine students' learning, so she had always opted for an exam-free classroom. Instead, SP used writing and research instead of standardized exams. The PRT Institute helped SP push that design approach even further, starting with a Real Talk and then building a connection to the class's final paper. In her asynchronous web class, she created a prerecorded Real Talk that discussed her struggle with education. SP expressed that it was nerve-wracking posting a video that felt so personal without a live audience to experience it with, and also that she has rerecorded it each of the three semesters she has taught since being involved in the Institute to make improvements. However, each semester the student response has been excellent.

In her Real Talk, SP described frustration with her inability to express herself in school and that most classes depended on memorization for success and didn't provide space to explore individual interests and goals. After this explanation, she transitioned the video into a conversation about the final paper. In the video, she encouraged students to consider their learning strengths (Are they strong writers? Would they express their learning better via audio recording? Would a video showcase their work best?), their interests, and their future goals. She posted her Real Talk video in a standard weekly announcement with the assignment, the grading rubric, and the timeline. This

Real Talk, paired with the overall enhancement of student belonging in the course, left students feeling comfortable to ask questions about the final paper that they had not asked before. Additionally, unlike semesters without Real Talk, SP has received several requests each semester from students who want to meet with her to discuss the paper together. The requests to meet and discuss the paper are particularly exciting because there are no required meetings for this class; more students opting to take time to talk through the assignment is a positive outcome. Students requesting meetings like this means SP is successfully removing the anonymity of an online course and building a community where students feel connected, are engaged, and are willing to ask questions.

With 10 years of teaching experience, SP expressed that all of these reactions have reenergized her in her classes. Asynchronous online classes can easily be isolating for both teachers and students, but SP's new approach has opened space to get to know her students and be a bigger part of their success. Reflecting upon the training experience, SP shared that the PRT Institute and Real Talk specifically helped her classroom become more inclusive and open in a way she had not thought of before. Additionally, she shared it has become clear that PRT's deliberate and focused approach creates a more intentional and robust classroom that enhances a student's sense of belonging.

With this particular example of Real Talk, the focus was establishing connections with students and tying it into the classwork students had to do. SP could have simply focused on connecting with students. As discussed previously, Real Talk is flexible. Teachers must use their discretion to determine whether to focus Real Talk on connections, curriculum, or both. That decision must be based on what the class needs from the Real Talk.

In the appendices, there are diverse sets of examples to help teachers see the different ways in which they can use Real Talk. It is a systematic way to establish successful and consistent connections with students on multiple levels in the classroom to help them succeed. Instead of being a one-dimensional approach, Real Talk has been purposefully designed to reinvigorate and motivate students and teachers.

It is through establishing connections with students at-promise that we begin the process of building their receptiveness to learning the material they must comprehend to succeed in school. Real Talk allows this to happen successfully throughout the semester in a deliberate yet authentic manner. Through Real Talk, teachers gain insight and understanding into students' terministic screens; it is the most effective and reliable approach within the pedagogy to do so. As teachers use these discussions strategically throughout the semester, students reveal the person behind the student every time. Real Talk affects and solidifies the connections between teachers and students at-promise. However, because Real Talks are such powerful tools, teachers should not use them every day. Instead, to sustain connections and relationships with students, teachers should use the information in the following chapter to supplement Real Talks.

NOTES

10 Professional Development

Alternative Lessons

In the next phase of training, teachers must then relate whatever subjects are important in their students' lives and/or life experiences to the curricular material, formulating lessons and discussions to reach out to those characteristics. It is crucial to maintain interconnectedness between each lesson and the core academic concepts. Although creating unique classroom lessons is not a new concept, engaging an entire class of learners at-promise is extraordinary. By applying the fundamental concepts of PRT, practically any lesson can entice students to be involved and establish receptiveness to learning from their teachers if it is based on students' terministic screens. Teachers will rely on these alternative lessons daily throughout their courses. They are crucial in sustaining student engagement, eagerness, and dedication to learning in between the strategically placed Real Talks. Thus, alternative lessons are a wonderful complement to Real Talk and the connections established with students in the classroom.

As we defined earlier, alternative lessons combine the content standard(s) from the curriculum with either the terministic screens of the students or societal issues outside of the classroom that will connect with students' terministic screens or resonate with them on a personal level. Through the creation and implementation of these lessons, teachers can create more encompassing connections to class material and sustain and complement the connections they have made with Real Talk. Using a step-by-step guide in this chapter and three examples from different teachers that show their alternative lessons, teachers should be able to create their own.

The appendices also contain several alternative lessons created by other teachers.

Any time we are delivering lessons to our students, we run the risk of alienating them, as we can easily fall into the trap of talking at the class and causing students to become disengaged from what we are attempting to teach them. Additionally, we also face the challenge that students do not see the material we are attempting to teach them as relevant; in some cases, students are simply intimidated by the seemingly complex material they must learn. These are common and everyday scenarios within classrooms in all educational institutions. But through alternative lessons, we are able to effectively overcome these barriers.

The process in creating an alternative lesson is simple but not simplistic and, as with Real Talk, I am offering the steps as a guide. Ultimately, educators will decide what steps are most useful for them.

1. Analyze the concept(s) you must teach your students.

2. Determine how the concept(s) can be connected to students' terministic screens or real-life situations.

3. Begin a comprehensive search for visuals, video clips, unique articles, pictures, and so on. If you do not use visual aids, be sure to pose clear scenarios and questions to students.

4. Piece together all the information to create an alternative lesson around the concept(s) or standard(s) students must learn.

5. Determine how you will assess student learning and determine effectiveness of the lesson.

6. Use your alternative lesson with your students.

Step 1

Begin by analyzing the concept or standard that the students must learn. By this, I mean that we cannot take for granted that we know the material we must teach our students. We must assess our own understanding of what we must teach our students critically to clearly see how to begin to creatively connect the material with our students. Additionally, in some cases, we are tasked to teach subjects that we are not so familiar with. Whether it's a new class, a class we have not taught in a long time, or something we are simply not well versed in—whatever the reason, these types of situations require our attention to make sure we analyze all the concepts we must teach our students. Our in-depth understanding of what we must teach will better serve our teaching the material to students.

Step 2

You cannot build or create an alternative lesson until you view the curriculum content and find a way to fuse the material with the students' terministic screens, what you have learned about them overall, or real-life events that will resonate with them. You can do this by reflecting on what you have learned about your students through Real Talks, dialogue, and all the other techniques used to gain insight into students. Also, you can use yourself and your life experiences when you feel that you do not have enough information gathered from students' terministic screens or experiences. This step is a reflection of what you have learned about your students. For new classes whose students you have not yet met, you must rely on real-life events that are in the media, popular culture, or anything else that will help you bring to life the concepts you are attempting to teach your students. Rather than ignore what is happening beyond the concrete walls of your classroom, bring the outside world into the classroom and connect it to what they must learn.

Step 3

In this step, you should simply conduct a search on the internet or perhaps sort through books, articles, newspapers, and so on to find the appropriate material that you would like to use within your alternative lesson. Take your time to do a comprehensive search. This will lead you to find as much relevant material as possible, but it will also allow you to make sure you are using credible and appropriate material. Once you have collected the material you will use for your alternative lesson, you move on to the next step.

Step 4

At this point, you have collected all of the different material you have decided to use. Now you combine everything to create the alternative lesson. You fuse the concept or standard, the terministic screens of your students or real-life events, and the material you decided to use from your search. You have now created an alternative lesson.

Step 5

Before you deliver an alternative lesson, you must determine what rubric you will use or create to assess student learning in your classroom. This step is specific to the needs of individual teachers and the manner in which they are asked to assess their students' progress. Assessing the success of your students through the alternative lesson is crucial to successfully show the growth that they have experienced.

Some examples are teachers who distribute a quiz, a test, writing assignment, or any other type of assignment to measure how well students learned and understood the concept(s) or standards within the alternative lesson. In other cases, teachers simply give a cumulative exam or project that students must complete after several days or weeks of the teacher having used alternative lessons. Ultimately, you should use whatever best serves you, your students, and the school's needs.

Step 6

After having completed the steps to create an alternative lesson, you are now ready to deliver it in your classroom. Remember to keep a few things in mind regarding an alternative lesson. Be creative and do not restrict yourself, but use discretion as you create these lessons. Alternative lessons are about not simply the creation but also the delivery. Alternative lessons can begin seemingly far removed from the content that students must learn, but eventually, they connect directly to what students must learn in class. There is also no specific length of time that you should adhere to. They can be 10, 15, 20, or 30 minutes long, and in some cases, they can even be delivered over the course of days or weeks. If students find the material relevant, are engaged, and feel connected to the teacher, they will be far more receptive to learning and in turn become more successful in school compared to when these components are missing in the teacher–student relationship.

Alternative Lesson Examples

In this section, I have added examples from three different content-area teachers who created their own alternative lessons. The diversity among alternative lessons should be clear in this section, along with the uniqueness of each one. But overall, they all share the foundation required to create alternative lessons. The manner in which each teacher begins and delivers the alternative lesson varies, but they all have shared that their students were receptive and engaged, learned the necessary material effectively, and did not demonstrate the typical resistance they were historically known to offer.

U.S. History: Discrimination

The following example shows how a teacher created an alternative lesson for her U.S. history class. She began the process by brainstorming what she had learned about her students through Real Talk. She identified a list of things she had learned that she could potentially fuse with the unit on the civil rights movement: discrimination, prejudice, unequal treatment, and bias. She eventually selected unequal treatment as the starting point and began to find ways to connect it to the students' terministic screens and eventually to the civil rights movement.

She then used the internet to gather additional ideas. She was careful with the information she gathered, ensuring that it was from reliable sources. In addition to internet sources (e.g., YouTube clips, pictures, media articles, academic journal articles), she searched in books, articles, autobiographies, photographs, and anything else she found compelling.

After all of her searching, this teacher used a test she had in her collection of resources from a 1996 edition of *Social Education*. The article included a lesson teachers could use in their social studies classes on the injustice of the Alabama literacy tests created in the 1960s to disenfranchise the African American population (*Social Education*, 1996). The test was one of the actual exams administered to potential voters in Alabama during that time and had been purposely created to be nearly impossible for African Americans to pass, thus keeping them from voting. Her objective was to help students understand and feel in a small way the frustration and injustice of these tests.

She used this existing lesson but put her own spin on it by making subtle changes to bring her students' terministic screens to the forefront of the lesson. She did not focus on voting as the original lesson did but rather on test taking. She knew her students had a negative perspective on tests and disliked them for a multitude of reasons. Thus, although she used an existing resource as the framework, she took the lesson in a different direction to create her own alternative lesson.

When she began the lesson, she first tapped into her students' terministic screens by having them write a response to this prompt: "Think of a time when you were treated unfairly and explain what happened." Starting the lesson in this manner allowed students to reveal their terministic screens as they wrote about being treated unfairly. She then moved to the next step in her lesson. As her students were writing, she abruptly stopped them and announced, "Oh! I forgot you have a test we need to take. So put your answers aside for now and get ready for the test." Her students were shocked by the statement because they had taken a unit test the previous day. Her students responded with typical resistance, ranging from passive aggressiveness, anger, and frustration to challenging her rationale for having to take another test. She simply said, "Just take the exam because we have talked about this, so you should know it." She also let them know that if they did not take the test, she might lower their grade by an entire letter grade. This forcefully encouraged students to take the test. Even though the students took the exam, she still encountered some resistance from students who vocalized their discontent: "This is not fair." She then added to their being upset by announcing that they had only 20 minutes to complete the exam, which consisted of 60 questions.

At the end of the time limit, she collected the tests and announced that she would let them know by the end of the day what they had scored. As she tried to move on to another topic, her students immediately resisted her, not allowing her to teach as they continued to speak about how upset they were about the impromptu test. Not letting things get out of control, she moved to the next part of her alternative lesson and immediately addressed the test: "It is a fake test. It will not count." Her students immediately made the connection to the writing prompt she had initiated earlier when she smiled and asked, "So what did I just do to all of you?" Her students shared that they felt they were being discriminated against because they were students who were at the mercy of the teacher. They felt helpless in being forced to do something they felt was unfair.

She then asked, "How did it feel to be treated unfairly by someone who has more power than you in a particular setting?" This led to intense dialogue regarding the topic of being treated unfairly, which she connected to discrimination in society. Having an open, receptive, and amicable discussion on discrimination was not a common occurrence in her class. This topic in her course was usually very challenging because many of the students resisted acknowledging societal disparities between racial groups. Some of her students were not interested because they viewed racial discrimination as a thing of the past; others simply shut down because they did not want to discuss the topic. Her students came from a rural area, and her class overwhelmingly consisted of one racial group, thus little racial diversity existed. Although I cannot determine if her students were racially biased or not based on the information she shared, the topic of race was challenging for them, as it is for many students, teachers, and people within the United States. Through this alternative lesson, the teacher helped her students become receptive to the unit on the civil rights movement by bringing discrimination to the forefront of her students' minds.

Although many of her students connected the content to themselves, teachers cannot simply assume that students will make connections to their own lives. Teachers must always be prepared to guide students if they need help to make the connections. In this case, the teacher asked her students how they personally felt about the unfair test and guided those who struggled to make the connection immediately.

Ultimately, this alternative lesson was extremely powerful. It struck a chord with students because they felt powerlessness, isolation, and unequal treatment within their own lives. The students realized that what was being asked of them in their class and what they needed to comprehend were actually connected to larger societal issues. The key was to show them the connection between what they were learning and their own terministic screens, personal experiences, and material that resonated with them on a personal level. Her alternative lesson took about 30 minutes, but the teacher shared that "it made a personal connection and resonated with them, leaving a lasting impression, and led to their receptiveness of the civil rights movement unit."

Mathematics: Building Bridges

A math teacher in an inner-city school, considered to be one of the lowest-performing schools within its state and the country, openly shared her challenges. She shared that her school was extraordinarily challenging for her as a first-year teacher. Culturally, she struggled as a middle-class white teacher in a predominantly African American, poverty-stricken community. She also shared that her administration was not supportive and that her students were not interested in what was being taught in her classrooms. However, this teacher was determined and extraordinarily dedicated to her students. As she was trained and developed in PRT, she showed she was very talented in creating alternative lessons for a subject matter that students struggled with tremendously.

Through a Real Talk, she learned that her students were interested in being recognized and acknowledged for having accomplished something significant within their lives. Although this may seem trivial to some, this was a major breakthrough for any teacher in her school, as there were no other teachers who were able to gather this type of personal insight from her students. She used the information she learned from her students by creating an alternative lesson. This alternative lesson is what helped her overcome the challenge of teaching a geometry class to students who were simply not interested in learning anything about the subject.

She decided to focus on center of mass and gravity, symmetry and the power of triangles, and stability for her alternative lesson. She knew the concepts very well and decided that the best way to connect them to her students was to have them build something in her class. She searched the internet and focused on YouTube videos to show her class. The first set of videos she decided to use was of different bridges collapsing; the next video was a news report of people "planking" (Channel 10, 2011)—lying face down with hands touching the sides of the body, sometimes in an unusual location. Lastly, she showed students how to use an interactive website to build shapes (Symmetry Artist, 2017).

After having conducted her search, she decided to use the videos of bridges collapsing as her initial "hook" to generate students' interest in her alternative lesson. After this, she would ask her students if they were interested in breaking a world record. Her focus was to have student teams build bridges out of Popsicle sticks and to see how much weight the bridges could withstand before they broke. She would follow this by sharing that their goal was to set a world record by competing against one another with the bridges they built. Her alternative lesson became multiple alternative lessons with the ultimate goal of reaching the final lesson of having them build their bridges. But before building bridges, students had to learn the concepts involved in building a bridge. This meant that they would have to learn about center of mass and gravity, symmetry and the power of triangles, and stability.

She separated each of the concepts into what she called mini lessons. This whole process happened over the course of five school days: The mini lessons were conducted over the course of two days, the building of the bridges took two days, and the weight test was conducted on the fifth day. Every mini lesson students had to do was clearly connected to the ultimate goal of building their bridge and establishing a world record. She also had rubrics built into the lessons to determine if the students were learning the material for her geometry class.

When she felt ready to deliver her alternative lesson, she did so by first asking her students if they had ever witnessed a bridge collapse. As she asked her question, she had her videos ready to show the class. As she showed the videos, her students were instantaneously engaged as they laughed and expressed amazement at the videos. (Like many other students at-promise, her students would laugh at things that were generally considered more serious than humorous in nature.) She used their engagement as the opportunity to ask them the question whether they were interested in breaking a world record by building a bridge made out of Popsicle sticks that could withstand an enormous amount of weight. Her students responded with excitement and eagerness. She shared with the class that they would first have to learn what it takes to build a strong bridge, and as soon they were done learning this, they would apply what they learned by building their own bridges. Her students agreed and were ready for what they needed to learn.

Her first mini lesson focused on center of mass and gravity. Before beginning the lesson, she showed students a short news report on planking to begin the discussion and work on center of mass and gravity. Her students were intrigued by the video, as it was a current fad within popular culture, and students knew about it. After a brief discussion, she moved on to the next part of the lesson. She had a series of objects for students to interact with and asked the students to find the center of mass for each. She kept them engaged by having them work with their hands, which also kept them interested and prevented them from becoming frustrated, as they were eager to get to the larger goal of building their bridges. Additionally, she also had students become involved physically by having them use their bodies in the process of attempting to figure out their own center of mass and gravity. Lastly, she had students determine stability by exploring various building/bridge designs and examining 3D shapes to determine how buildings/bridges become stable (see Appendix M for all of her mini lessons).

Her second mini lesson was on symmetry and the power of the triangle. Before she had her students begin their work, she reminded them again of the importance of the work they would be doing that day in making sure they would build strong bridges that could withstand large amounts of weight. As she began the work, her first step was having students go to the Math Is Fun website (Symmetry Artist, 2017) to use something interactive to design symmetric shapes. Once they created the shapes, she had students explain why symmetry is important to a bridge. Additionally, she had them explore why triangles are important to building bridges and other structures. She had students build different shapes with cardstock and fasteners that included shapes with triangles and without triangles, and students applied force to the shapes to determine the weakest points. Ultimately, students connected everything they learned back to their bridges, as their next step was now to begin the process of building their bridge.

She had her students do something that was also unusual and difficult within her school. She had students work in groups as they began building their bridges. Working in groups was not common in her school. Students struggled to work independently, and to work in groups usually meant chaos or even fights among students. But in this case, the teacher had absolutely no problems with her students working together. In fact, they worked so well together and she was so proud of them that she took pictures of her students while they worked in teams to design and build their bridges. The final steps students took were designing their bridges in their groups; creating a "college report" that included their objective, materials, hypothesis, and procedure; their calculations of how many Popsicle sticks they would need; their analysis, conclusion, and revision and reflection; and, lastly, their peer-to-peer evaluation. Although this process may seem tedious on paper, it took little time to create but paid dividends within her classroom.

On the day students finished building their bridges and the competition began, involvement went well beyond engaging that one class in the alternative lesson. Her students had been so excited and proud that they'd discussed what they were doing in her class with many other students and teachers in the school. Students from other classes asked their teachers' permission to witness the bridges being tested, and many were allowed to attend. As the teams began putting weights on their bridges—one bridge at a time until it finally broke—they were cheered on and encouraged by the audience that had filled the classroom to be a part of this day. Not only were her own students engaged from beginning to end, but students from other classes also asked to be in her class to do similar types of assignments. Students learned an enormous amount of information that they needed for their geometry class, but they *and* their visitors had fun, were engaged, saw the work as relevant, and were invested in their learning process. The bridge that ultimately won the competition was able to withstand 145 pounds; they ran out of weights to further test the bridge, and it did not break.

The math teacher's alternative lesson varies tremendously from the history teacher's lesson, and you will notice the same for the Spanish teacher's alternative lesson in the final example.

Spanish: Stereotypes

The Spanish teacher worked in an inner-city school that was almost 100 percent African American within a community steeped in poverty. His school was considered low performing, in which fewer than 60 percent of students graduated from high school. He also initially struggled to connect with his students; as a middle-class white teacher, he admittedly found it difficult to connect with his students, who seemed so different from him. As he progressed in his semester, he slowly but surely began to connect with his students through Real Talk and other methods he found useful in his class. As he connected with his students, he still faced a difficult challenge. His students admittedly shared with him that they had no interest in Spanish; in fact, they did not appreciate having to learn it because they saw no use for it. The Spanish teacher was in part able to overcome this with a combination of alternative lessons and through the connection he made with his students to teach them the relevancy of being, at the very least, bilingual in the global society that we live in. But his first step was generating an interest in what he was teaching in class.

Ultimately, the Spanish teacher was tasked to teach students how to understand and speak basic Spanish. But he also felt it was important for students to understand the cultural diversity and individual cultures found within the Spanish-speaking countries. This led to one of his first alternative lessons, focusing on the unit that needed to be covered on clothing, but he also decided to teach students about the diversity among the Latinx population beyond the stereotypical views some people have within the United States.

As he assessed what he had to teach them and felt comfortable in his understanding of it, he immediately began to think of his students' terministic screens. He knew that his students struggled with being young African Americans who are stereotyped within society. He embedded this insight into his alternative lesson. He then moved on and began his search on the internet to look for images he would use in his alternative lesson. As he searched, he decided that he would highlight the diversity in phenotypes among Latinx. As he picked the different people he would use, he decided to use images of them in different styles of dress, such as professional and casual attire. He also decided to pick different Spanish magazines that he would bring to class to have students work with as well. Once he had all of this information, he was able to put it together to create his alternative lesson. He ultimately brought all of his material together through a PowerPoint to show the visuals and present his alternative lesson to his class. Lastly, his method of assessing students was to have them speak in Spanish to one another on the subject matter and to write their thoughts in Spanish as well.

As he began the lesson in his class he asked, "What do you imagine when you think of a Spanish speaker?" He immediately asked them to write down three ways to describe the person they imagined. As they finished writing their responses, he asked students to share some of their responses. He allowed students to openly share their responses for a few minutes before he moved on by asking them what they based their responses on. He asked if they were based on personal experience, television, movies, the internet, and so on. As students responded, he brought up his PowerPoint on the projector for students to see. As their attention turned toward the PowerPoint, he began to explain what he would be sharing with them.

He asked the class to focus on the pictures he was going to show them and to share if they thought the individual was Latinx or was not, as well as guess the individual's profession. The pictures he showed them were not titled. The pictures were of Victor Cruz (professional football player), Saul "Canelo" Alverez (professional boxer), Carlos Slim (billionaire businessman), Alexis Bledel (actress), Sofia Vergara (actress), Cameron Diaz (actress), and Peter Gene Hernandez, better known as Bruno Mars (singer–songwriter). As they went through the pictures, students recognized some but ultimately struggled with determining who was Latinx.

As they finished going through the PowerPoint, they discussed as a class the diversity among Latinx and the stereotypes associated with how people look. He further connected people being stereotyped to what students in class had shared in the past, and he gave them an opportunity to share what it felt like to be stereotyped. Students shared openly and felt connected to what he was teaching about

Latinx and the Spanish language. As he moved on from what people looked like and the stereotypes associated with them, he introduced them to the topic of clothing. He asked them to share their thoughts on one aspect of "code-switching," when people wear professional clothing versus casual clothing. As students began to discuss this, he divided students into groups and handed out magazines that were in Spanish for them to use. He asked students to pick clothing within the magazines, describe and discuss the clothing together, and write summaries of their thoughts on the clothing—all in Spanish.

His students were engaged with this alternative lesson and found it relevant, as the connection was initially made through stereotypes and made the entire process interactive for students so they would take part. For a group of students who, at face value, did not seem interested in learning or participating in their Spanish class, this teacher was able to engage them, generate an interest, and teach them the material they needed to learn. Overall, his alternative lesson took 35 minutes in his class and was, according to the teacher, easy to create.

These three examples of alternative lessons highlight the diversity found among alternative lessons. They are unique to each teacher, yet they all share the same fundamental foundation.

Alternative lessons take very little time to create and can have a major impact on the learning process for students. Creating alternative lessons can also be fun—quite different from the dreadful feeling that accompanies the time and work teachers put into traditional lesson plans that may yield little, if any, return. As mentioned earlier, as educators we sometimes become complacent with our own academic and personal growth. Alternative lessons help break through these barriers because they force us to grow continually on multiple levels. More important is their ability to help us expand our knowledge base: We simply learn more as we create alternative lessons for our students. This constant learning further benefits our students because, as we grow, we can share what helps us grow with our students. That, in turn, helps them find ways to grow continually as well. Alternative lessons not only are fun to create but also take little time to generate. Implementing them maximizes positive outcomes in class because alternative lessons are the perfect complement to Real Talk, building and sustaining teachers' connectedness and success with their students over time.

New Beginnings 11

For far too long, our schools have been plagued with a dropout epidemic. We cannot afford to let millions of students drop out of school each year. We cannot simply give up on students at-promise or blame them for the circumstances that have contributed to their rejection of traditional school cultures. As professionals, we are responsible for finding ways to reach every student entrusted to our care, not just the ones who are easy to teach or who learn what we set before them easily. Our challenge is to reach the seemingly unreachable. But no student is completely unreachable. It just takes one teacher willing to go beyond the usual parameters of traditional pedagogy to make the difference in a student's life. We must remember that it is the students who need us the most who will push us away the most.

I spent my entire K–12, community college, and university experience identified as a student at-promise. When I found a teacher that I felt truly connected with, I performed well in class. I had the ability, but my life circumstances, my rejection of school norms, my not seeing anything relevant in what was being taught, and my lack of meaningful connections with teachers caused me to feel that school was a place for everyone except me. I felt like an impostor sitting in my classes, that my rightful place was in the streets. Teachers did not understand the hatred I had for school. Adding to my isolation, I'd been taught to show no signs of weakness and not to ask questions. I was not unique in this sense; a population of students who shared my sentiments and were at risk of dropping out of school existed decades before me, and they will exist decades after me. These experiences, however, were the foundation for creating something not only fundamentally sound but also infused with passion that can increase passing rates for students at-promise. Rather than highlighting the timeless epidemic of students at-promise dropping out of school and feeling overwhelmed by it, I chose to create a timeless approach to help reduce this epidemic.

Simply teaching students and having them learn may work for teachers of the college-bound students. These students adapt to teachers, curriculum, subjects, rules, and lessons because they accept that they must do these things to be successful in school. Students at-promise do not adjust in this manner, which results in an adversarial relationship with teachers and schools. Overcoming this kind of relationship becomes very difficult when teachers receive more and more students at-promise into their classroom, many of whom have made up their minds not to like their teachers before even meeting them.

After working with thousands of educators, I have come to realize how very isolating teaching in the classroom can be. Many of us know this, but we seldom discuss it. Although we work in institutions alongside colleagues, once we enter the arena of our classrooms, we face the overwhelming task of teaching a large group of students on a day-to-day basis. The pressure is immense. As days turn into months, the isolation we feel as educators in the American education system solidifies. Given the rigors of teaching, we can easily become complacent. But it is crucial for us to resist. Complacency will only hurt both the students and us, the teachers, in the classroom.

Breaking through the constraints of complacency is complicated by the highly personal nature of pedagogy. Teaching is a personal craft, an art form, and a science. Because it is so personal, some people have difficulty accepting that they need to improve or possibly completely revamp what they do in their classrooms. We must accept that, as human beings, we will always have opportunities to grow and improve. Being educators is no different. The most successful educators I have met were willing to accept their need for growth in certain areas and searched for ways to improve their teaching continually to increase the performance and passing rates of their most challenging students.

Any educator willing to build connections with students and to adapt to meet the needs of their students can use PRT in any subject area. Educators of any student-at-promise population can implement PRT to help their students succeed. At the core of PRT is the breaking down of socially constructed barriers and the establishing of meaningful connections between educators and students. Creating honest and open communication between educators and their students, giving students a voice in shaping their classroom environments, and allowing students to teach their teachers as they are taught by their teachers empower students to learn. However, the ability to relate to students is a skill that is not easily taught. Only through actual face-to-face or virtual interactions with students can educators establish such relatedness.

Educators must also be willing to stray from their comfort zone and take a genuine interest in their students' lives while sharing components of their own lives to begin to build relationships with students. Understanding that students are people before they are students is essential in establishing meaningful connections. Making connections with students is not a one-dimensional approach in which students share and educators merely listen. Rather, it is a process whereby students can comfortably feel and say that they know who their teacher is as a person, thus establishing and recognizing effective relationships. As educators begin sincerely and effectively to relate to their students at-promise, they will create opportunities to learn about their students' terministic screens. By using students' terministic screens to create dynamic lessons that maximize student engagement, educators can build the connections needed to reach their students. Integral to this process are the Real Talk discussions.

Real Talk is very powerful and can be used on its own or in unison with the pedagogy in its entirety to maximize its effectiveness. However, mastering Real Talk is a process. Educators must be both patient and willing to learn how to use it effectively in their classrooms. Although Real Talk is one of the most challenging pieces in the pedagogy, over the years I have witnessed educators who have learned to use it appropriately to transform not only the lives of their students but their own lives as well. Many of the educators I worked with truly had a passion to help their students. However, they simply were not finding the tools they needed to realize their passion. Real Talk is a tool educators can use to achieve success in a manner many educators no longer believe is possible. Many of these educators feel it is impossible to establish meaningful connections with their students that will result in improving the performance of their students at-promise. Thus, with Real Talk, educators revitalize themselves and their careers.

Establishing success from semester to semester is something that only strengthens the approach. Educators achieve this continual success by adapting the pedagogy to meet the needs of their students and their classes. Adaptability is not a unique characteristic of this teaching style. It is a skill that any willing educator with a drive to engage students can incorporate. Many students at-promise around the country have difficulty seeing the relevancy, importance, or connection of the material educators want them to learn. Their lack of connection with their teachers also stands in their way of learning. Educators accept education as a long-term investment for success and may not fathom the idea of rejecting school. Students at-promise, however, are more entrenched in their present and the difficulties they face in their daily lives. They may have difficulty imagining or understanding how their education will affect the next 20 years of their lives. By being adaptable, educators will understand their students better, enabling them to find avenues through which they can help students adopt education as a form of empowerment within their lives. In fact, when instructors are willing, the students themselves will often express their need for adaptation and will contribute ideas for restructuring lessons to make them more effective.

It's not a common practice for teachers to consistently engage students at-promise in the learning process. For many students, learning school material is a tedious process. This tedium is even more pronounced for students who reject school norms, as many students at-promise do. PRT allows educators to repair the damage done to so many of these students. Through this pedagogy, we can let our students know who we are and that we care about them, about who they are, and about what they need to survive and to rise above their circumstances. We can prepare them to overcome any future inequality they may encounter. We can teach them not only to be successful in our classes but also to embrace education, preparing them for the academic challenges they will face in the future. Helping students at-promise transform from rejecting school to embracing it is a monumental accomplishment for any educator. It is a humbling experience to witness students willing to learn and having fun in the classroom without feeling disdain toward learning.

Dread, intimidation, and feelings of hopelessness do not have to exist for educators who work with students at-promise. Throughout my years of teaching, working with educators, and in having been a student at-promise, I have witnessed countless passionate educators become jaded, almost cynical, as the daily grind of teaching disengaged students wore them down. To see the light of passion in teachers' eyes again and to bring that passion to the forefront of their teaching is transforming not only for the teachers but also for their students. The disadvantaged backgrounds of some students at-promise do not have to result in their academic disadvantage in the classroom. By developing inclusive, structured, student-oriented learning environments and incorporating methods and strategies to build better connections with students, educators can reach students at-promise and help them achieve academically. We can help them become successful, fulfilled, productive members of society. PRT is designed to do just that. I encourage all educators to begin implementing PRT in classrooms today. Start small, but start. Break down the barriers that prevent educators and students from reaching high levels of success together.

Time is too precious to wait for the next semester or the next school year. Too many passionate, highly skilled teachers are drowning in classes where they are trying so desperately to help their students succeed. Teachers are feeling pressure from administrators and city, state, and federal governments to stop the elevated dropout rates. Rather than sit and argue about who is to blame for these dropout rates, teachers must be the first to take action, to lead by example as we slowly but surely garner the support of the education system. We must be willing to incorporate viable approaches to bolster our success in the classroom.

PRT can be that approach. Educators who are already practicing some components of the approach can adopt the remaining components to fill the gaps in their pedagogical repertoire. Educators currently using approaches that are quite different from PRT can choose to adopt this new pedagogy instead, completely revamping their teaching approach. Time is of the essence. Students at-promise don't have time to waste, and we cannot allow students to continue to drop out of school.

As I reflect on the creation and implementation of PRT, I can't help but smile as I see the faces of the numerous students I have had the privilege of serving directly or indirectly through the educators who are using the approach. I am always filled with excitement as I walk into classrooms filled with students at-promise. They remind me that coming up with a pedagogical game plan is easy for individuals far away from the classroom; it is another thing entirely to be the person in the classroom who has to implement the approach with a group of uninterested students. Every educator has a game plan before walking into the classroom, but it only takes a few minutes with a group of students at-promise before the educator is tossing that plan out the window. PRT was not created in a room or an office far removed from the classrooms of students at-promise. It took form thanks to the teachers and students who informed and sharpened its uniqueness, applicability, and success. PRT is a solid fundamental base yet is purposely flexible to allow educators to adapt to the uniqueness of every person willing to use it with their students. Any pedagogy created without taking the uniqueness of each individual and the differences between people into account will be too rigid to be successful with all students. PRT is a flexible tool that will work for all types, styles, and personalities of educators who are sincerely willing to try it and who strive to grow.

Our work to adapt and adopt new teaching strategies is, of course, about student success. This focus is our mission. However, the crux of this work is about us—educators, administrators, and educational support staff. Recently, I attended a meeting where a colleague eloquently and passionately stated that students should be at the center of our decisions, and I agree wholeheartedly. Students are not the "issue" when it comes to lagging student success. Instead, the challenges and struggles with student success are related to "us." If teachers choose not to make changes in the classroom, then new pedagogical approaches, initiatives, state or federal recommendations, and more data proving what is and is not effective in the classroom is meaningless. I am not referring to teachers who go above and beyond to invest in finding ways to improve in the classroom. Instead, I am referring to obstructionist teachers who use their privileged positions to refuse and resist changes and blame students for failure. Students suffer the most when we allow these ineffective teachers to impede education; there is no room in education for those who are unwilling to accept their role in student success.

Administrators also play a role. Too many administrators obstruct and lack a commitment to developing and supporting teachers in the classroom. Self-absorbed, incompetent administrators who subjugate teachers, are spiteful, and create fear amongst colleagues directly obstruct student success. Destructive administrators stifle the atmosphere necessary to teach educators how to use PRT and institutionalize the PRT method. More importantly, dysfunctional administrators demoralize teachers, which negatively impacts students. There is also no room for these administrators in education. One of the best pieces of advice I received in the Aspen Rising Presidents Fellowship is from a retired and highly successful higher-education leader who said, "Great leaders have tough skin and a big heart." Administrators are responsible for creating cultures where teachers feel and think anything is possible by working collaboratively.

My hope is that educators, students, school districts, and society will all benefit from the success we can establish in the classroom for a population of students for whom success has been elusive for many generations. I am hopeful that, based on what I have provided, people not only will find the pedagogy useful and sustainable over time but also will improve on it whenever possible. Pedagogy is a constantly evolving process that must continually grow within the hearts and minds of the individuals who practice it in their classrooms. This constant growth will only further contribute to the success of those we ultimately serve in our classrooms: our students. If I am fortunate, I will live to see this work further enhanced by the brilliant minds that exist in our world—perhaps by those of other students at-promise who not only beat the odds stacked against them but also set a new standard for how we view and value intellect within our society.

NOTES

Appendices

Appendix A:	Real Talk on Partnerships and an Alternative Lesson on Critical Thinking and Clinical Judgment	153
Appendix B:	Real Talk on Adversity and an Alternative Lesson on Chemical Bonding	156
Appendix C:	Real Talk on Doubt	159
Appendix D:	Real Talk on You Belong	162
Appendix E:	Real Talk on Symbolism	164
Appendix F:	"Who I Am" Real Talk on the First Day of Class	167
Appendix G:	Real Talk on Adversity	170
Appendix H:	Real Talk on Individuality in Learning	174
Appendix I:	Real Talk on Being Authentic	176
Appendix J:	Real Talk on Classroom Norms	178
Appendix K:	Examples of Real Talk Themes	180
Appendix L:	Bridge Project Packet	181
Appendix M:	Alternative Lesson on Congruent Triangles	192
Appendix N:	Alternative Lesson on Graphing Different Types of Linear Systems	199
Appendix O:	Alternative Lesson on Public Speaking Anxiety	206

Appendix A

Real Talk on Partnerships and an Alternative Lesson on Critical Thinking and Clinical Judgment

KH decided that she would apply her first Real Talk as part of her program's orientation. She focused her Real Talk around partnerships, specifically on how she wanted to develop partnerships with students to help them excel in her nursing program class. Her Real Talk focused on her experience as a nursing student, beginning with nursing orientation.

She began her orientation by welcoming the students and introducing herself. However, unlike past orientations, this time she paused after opening with "My name is Nurse. . . ." Instead, she added, "You know that still sounds strange to me when I say it out loud. I guess because, like you sitting here today, it brings me back to when I was sitting in your same place, nursing orientation." This slight shift set the stage for commonality as she moved into her Real Talk.

KH shared with students that despite the many years since she sat in the same course they were currently taking with her, the course was still called *Fundamentals of Nursing*, just as when she was a student. As she progressed, she reflected on her first day of nursing orientation and how she felt looking at the people around her who were also entering the nursing program. KH shared that she wondered at the time, "Who will be left by graduation?" With all she had heard and was hearing that day about the demands of the program and having to meet such high expectations, she thought, "Will *I* still be here at the end of the program?"

She shared her feelings of insecurity and how as orientation progressed, she listened to the professor talk about the course. She shared the feelings of doubt that continued to fill inside her and the lingering question, "Am I good enough to make it?" Explaining that she "did not have a crystal ball to look into to tell her where she would be today, never imagining that she would be standing in front of her students today." She went on to explain that if she "could have rolled the years forward and saw how it was going to play out, that, wow, that would have really put me at ease, but the reality was I had no idea."

After she shared her experience, she elaborated on how consuming her concerns of not succeeding in the nursing program were for her as a student; it took time away from enjoying the journey of learning and interfered with her ability to focus and study. She explained that even though this was a long time ago, she has never forgotten her experience as a nursing student.

She ended the Real Talk by saying, "So why do I share this with you?" She elaborated, "Because the standards, criteria, and rigor of the nursing program still remain to this day, along with high percentages and multiple timed tests you will have to perform throughout the entirety of the program. While the program is unchanged in some ways, teachers helped me get through the program, and I, too, will help you get through. I don't want you to waste time or energy unnecessarily worrying like I did. I take seriously ownership and responsibility to help you build your fundamental nursing foundation to successfully jumpstart you into the nursing program as you begin to care for patients within our community. We will do this together. Put in all of your effort, and I promise you I will put in all of my effort to make sure we begin a partnership that will ensure the future of your success."

As she concluded her sharing, KH asked the students if they had any questions. If they preferred, students could also ask her questions after orientation or at any point in the semester about what she had shared or anything else they thought she could help them with.

Alternative Lesson

KH created and implemented this alternative lesson for her first-semester nursing program students. The alternative lesson's purpose is to create and enhance nursing students' critical thinking and clinical judgment skills. The nursing students in this class were first introduced to these concepts as they relate to nursing interventions and patient-care. KH was using the alternative lesson to have the students demonstrate that there is more than one way of executing a task through critical thinking and clinical judgment. She wanted her students to have a way to understand what constitutes a higher level of thinking and using clinical judgment in caring and intervening for patients. Additionally, she wanted to focus on how reflecting on past experience builds efficiency and knowledge on what we continue to do, or not do, within the professional nursing practice. She chose for this alternative lesson to use a visual representation that she learned most students could relate to—a picture from the book *Where's Waldo*.

After explaining the definitions of critical thinking and clinical judgment, she shared a picture of Waldo. She first asked the students to find Waldo within the picture. Once a student had identified Waldo, she prompted that same student to identify the method used to find Waldo. Additionally, she inquired if the student had performed this exercise before. If so, she asked if he or she had used this same method during this exercise. She then discussed how patterns once used can be repeated to create efficiency and build their nursing knowledge. Lastly, she asked what other things about the picture did they see as they were performing the task, and did they learn anything about the situation or circumstances surrounding Waldo. If the students replied yes, she then explained how this lends to the process of critical thinking to make clinical judgments within their professional nursing practice.

She used this alternative lesson to teach students that, as nurses, they have many tasks. However, with these tasks come the responsibility to formulate more information about the situation to provide patient-centered care. She encouraged the students that they should not only focus on just the task at hand. She pointed out that if the focus is only on the task at hand, they should consider how much data will be missed that may have contributed to their clinical judgment and patient-centered nursing intervention(s). She also explained to students that they needed to be flexible and learn to adapt if needed, using their clinical judgment while attempting to execute a particular nursing intervention/task. She finished the alternative lesson by explaining how missing data could also lend to potential, avoidable, adverse patient outcomes.

Appendix B

Real Talk on Adversity and an Alternative Lesson on Chemical Bonding

DJ decided to conduct three different Real Talks over the semester. He did one on the first day of class, one in the middle of the semester, and a third two weeks before the end of the semester. The following Real Talk was conducted in the middle of the semester and is about adversity. He felt strongly about conducting this Real Talk after seeing his students struggle with different forms of adversity.

DJ's Real Talk consists of a story about his experience with adversity after making the wrong choice. He shares with students about a time he and some friends became stuck on a cliffside in the dark due to a wrong decision. They were not only stuck on a dangerously steep cliff, but they knew they could also inadvertently step on or bump into a venomous snake. A fun trip with friends quickly turned into a potentially life-threatening situation. He openly shares with the class how he felt alone, defeated, and guilty for endangering his friends' lives.

DJ conveys to the class that at that point he knew he had to decide how he would approach this situation. He could give up or come up with a plan to overcome the adversity he was facing. He explains to the class that he decided this situation would not be the end of his life or his friends' lives. They brainstormed and developed a plan to maneuver through the large rocks, thorned bushes, and other dangers. Eventually, they made it up and off the cliff. He shares that he was tired when he reached the top but felt a deep sense of relief and accomplishment that they had made it out safely.

Next, DJ relates things back to the middle of the semester when some students may feel fatigued and hopeless trying to complete the semester successfully. He also highlights how some of them may feel alone without any family support or may fear letting their families down by not succeeding in school. Finally, DJ circles back to his decision to persevere and push himself to make it to the top of that cliff, as he encourages them not to give up and continue to the end of the semester.

As he ends his Real Talk, DJ ensures students that they are not alone, that they have him as a guide and support—that if they are willing to talk with him, he will find a way to help them with their challenges. For DJ, the purpose of his Real Talk is to affirm for students that he is always there for them and will continue to help them throughout the rest of the semester and beyond.

Alternative Lesson

The instructor designed this alternative lesson for his biology classes. He noted that students struggle with biology topics. Additionally, the topics he teaches in class build on the previous processes, and making lessons fluid from one concept to the next can be challenging. One area of particular difficulty for students deals with chemical bonding, pH, and the interaction between different chemicals. DJ noticed his students were not engaged while he taught these concepts. To help alleviate this problem and increase engagement and fluidity between chemistry and an introduction to cell biology, the instructor developed an alternative lesson to incorporate soap and disease prevention.

To connect the alternative lesson more directly to students' lives, the instructor incorporates the current COVID-19 pandemic. Introducing this common experience allows students to explore the subject matter and connect it to their daily lives. Within the discussion, he purposefully includes chemistry through soap to clean and disinfect hands and surfaces for safety measures.

He then shares a video on handwashing from the Center for Disease Control. After the video's conclusion, he asks students what they found interesting in the video and to write down any questions the video inspired about how soap works and hand washing. The student's questions are then included in the lesson to help facilitate engagement with the topic.

Rather than only discussing soap, he asks his students to research on the internet to determine the ingredients of soap. Students discover that the typical components of soap include a base and some type of oil through this process. He then leads the class to determine what they need to know about chemistry to understand a base's characteristics.

The class then discusses atoms and chemical bonds to determine what type of bonds produce acids and bases. Once students have a good understanding of bonds, they determine why oil is used in soap making. Through this process, he ensures that students must understand the chemical structure of oil and how it interacts with water.

As part of the learning process in his alternative lesson and the discussion with students, he includes activities to help solidify the concepts. These activities involve examining liquids, solids, and gases when learning about atoms and their parts. Activities exploring pH are included to evaluate weak acids and bases and the pH of household items. He also includes activities evaluating oil and water interactions with salts to help students understand the difference between polar and nonpolar molecules.

Once students understand these concepts, they get a chance to make soap in class. The students get to use what they learned to describe what is happening while making soap. This lesson is conducted at the beginning of the semester to allow the soap to cure, and it also gives students something to look forward to at the end of the semester. At the end of the semester, students get to take home the handmade bar of soap they each made in class.

This alternative lesson keeps students engaged in a concept area that is typically difficult to understand. It also allows students to understand the reactions between everyday items, how they interact, and their chemical properties. He also creates a smooth transition from chemistry to the plasma membrane. Ultimately, students enjoy this alternative lesson while learning about the chemical reactions that go into the process of making soap.

Appendix C

Real Talk on Doubt

For this Real Talk, CH decided to focus on doubt. CH learned through her observation and interaction with students that doubt played a role in many students' lives. Whether doubt with success in school or doubting their abilities to have a successful career, CH realized it was a barrier for them. CH's written Real Talk follows.

Do you ever wonder if you have what it takes to be successful? Success is not something that happens overnight. Success develops over time. Some people are more successful at reaching their goals and dreams than others. And everyone is different and has their own story to share about their own personal journey. Some start off with more privilege than others. Others start off with less privilege, maybe coming from poverty or lack of family support or against other systemic barriers out of their control. But where people start in life does not have to define their future.

For me, I'm a first-generation college student. My parents were high school dropouts. Neither of them graduated from high school, and they also got married when they were teenagers. My mom was 17 when they got married, and they had their first child while she was a teenager. They knew nothing about how to navigate the college process, so they weren't able to help me either. I was a pretty good student in high school, though, and I knew I wanted to go to college.

When it came to apply, I only applied to one school—Pepperdine University in Malibu, California. I didn't know you were supposed to apply to more than one school! Luckily, I got in. My parents put me on a plane in Chicago and sent me off 1,200 miles to Los Angeles. I had never been on a plane before—I was excited and also scared to death! I figured out how to get from LAX to Malibu, and at first, I felt like a fish out of water. Everyone seemed so confident and beautiful. And I was not. I had no idea what I wanted to do with my life. I changed my major so many times. But my family's goal was for me to graduate from college, and I did! But there was no career plan for what I would do after I graduated. I graduated with a degree in sociology and had no idea what to do with that.

Over the years, I waited tables and hopped around different jobs in social work, working with kids who were wards of the court, with teen parents, with foster kids, with at-risk kids in the public schools, and with kids with behavioral issues. I worked two and three jobs at a time, and after about five years, I was frustrated that I wasn't advancing in my career. I was confused about why I was working so hard without it paying off. I remember driving in my car and yelling, "What's wrong with me? Why am I not getting anywhere?"

My family kept telling me I needed a mentor, so I looked for a mentor in education. I figured I needed to find someone like me—a white, older female who could understand my journey. I met with a few women, and they were nice, but it just didn't click. And then one day I was at an education conference. The emcee introduced the speaker, and he had a completely different background than my own. So up to the podium steps BW, a young man of color. He talked about struggles and heartache and disappointment and fear of striving for goals. He talked about wanting more and overcoming his fear of failure and about how he embraced his challenges as opportunities to grow rather than letting them defeat him and about how he worked so hard to overcome his circumstances. I could not relate to his exact experiences, but I could relate to his story because I had experienced those same feelings. And so I felt a connection to BW. The things he talked about made sense to me in terms of what he was trying to achieve in education, and the way he delivered his talk connected with me on an emotional level.

Eventually, I reached out to BW, and we began collaborating on some projects; over time, he became a mentor to me. Through that process, what I realized was that I was missing three things that were holding me back: strategy, mental toughness, and belief. As for strategy, I learned that hard work without strategy is useless. I was working three jobs at a time, but my efforts weren't focused toward an identified goal. BW taught me to formulate a strategy and to laser my focus. Concerning belief, I realized that being the daughter of high school dropouts, I had trouble seeing myself beyond the level that my parents had achieved in their careers. Not having much exposure to people in professional careers, I couldn't visualize myself rising the ranks in my professional life. BW told me he believed in me and that I needed to get my PhD. Who me? Was I smart enough? Would people laugh at me? And finally, with regard to mental toughness, I was raised to be sweet, polite, supportive, and accommodating, always putting my needs second. Can some of you relate to that? BW taught me to toughen up and to be assertive and not to let setbacks defeat me. I took all of that to heart and got to work.

That was 2015, and since then, I have gotten two promotions, started my PhD, published articles, lost 40 pounds, and started running. Unfortunately, I didn't get these messages until I was 50 years old. If I had gotten them when I was your age—if someone would have taught me about strategy and told me they believed in me so that I believed it and taught me how to frame my obstacles as opportunities to grow and learn when I was your age—who knows where I might be today.

So this is what I will tell you today. I believe in you. I believe in your ability to be successful in school, and you do belong here. You are tough. You can tackle your challenges head-on. Don't let your current circumstances or the way you see yourself or messages you have gotten from others about how you can't—or you shouldn't or you're not good enough—stop you. Get tough and believe in yourself. Come up with a strategy. Where do you want to be when you are 30, 40, 50 years old? Dream about that, imagine where you will live, what car you will drive, what you might do for a living, and then formulate your strategy and work backward. And part of your strategy should include education. Use education as the source to achieve your dreams and so you can set yourself up to change the world in a positive way for yourself, your family, your community, or in whatever way you think you should.

Does my story make sense to you? Can anyone relate to anything I've said that they would like to share?

Thank you for sharing. Remember, believe in yourself, work on developing mental toughness, and start thinking about a strategy for your future.

Appendix D

Real Talk on You Belong

This Real Talk took place in a one-on-one context with DL. I am not sharing the entirety of our dialogue. Instead, I am only sharing a part of my Real Talk. The point here is to show Real Talk's versatility and how you can use this method, whether with an entire classroom or in a one-on-one setting.

DL, you remind me of myself. I think of the younger version of me sitting across from me as you are now and how I wouldn't listen to anything I am about to say to you. I hope it is different with you and that you can hear what I am saying to you.

I didn't think I belonged in school or in any kind of career. In fact, I didn't think I was worthy of any opportunity to better my life. I wish I could go back in time and shake that younger version of me and say, "Absolutely, no doubt, you belong in college and have the right to earn a fulfilling career and life." But I can't go back in time, and luckily, I have an even better opportunity right now talking with you. I don't want you to feel what I felt or think what I thought back then.

This world needs you. It needs your unique experiences and perspective to make it a better place. You have value beyond what you can currently imagine, and not only can you live an amazing life, but you will help others live amazing lives too. Nothing in life is easy. Whether you choose to go to college or not go to college, life will always be challenging in some way. That is normal, and it is okay. What is not okay is thinking that you don't belong in college.

When you go to college, you may have days where you feel lonely, like you have no friends, and that people are out to "get you." You will get lost in your thoughts and doubt yourself. It will make you ask yourself, "Do I belong here?" The answer is simple: Yes, you do.

You belong in college as much as all of the other college students do. Don't get lost on how other students are doing and how they might be doing better than you—focus on you, your development, and how you can evolve. Stay in constant learner mode and learn from the people around you. Being a learner will serve you well in school, in your career, and in life.

DL, don't let people convince you that you are not capable. It is okay for people to doubt you. It is okay for people to give up on you. It is not okay for *you* to give up on you and for you not to believe in you. You have the opportunity and ability to make your dreams come true, but you are running the risk of not making that happen if you give up on yourself. DL, tell me, what's getting in your way, and what can I do to help?

NOTES

Appendix E

Real Talk on Symbolism

I had to create a Real Talk to introduce students to symbolism because it was a section of the reading component of the GED exam. This Real Talk was for a different class and group of students (than those discussed in Chapter 9) regarding adversity. I created it because the students were neither receptive to discussing symbolism nor aware of its importance. They wanted to skip this section, which many of them referred to as "stupid" or "boring." Because the students were struggling to understand symbolism based on their previous experiences, I also sensed an element of fear.

Therefore, I created a Real Talk that began by focusing on our lives and eventually connected to the symbolism section in the GED.

Teacher: Let me ask you all something very specific today. How has being away from home been since you have been here at MSU? I mean, specifically, how has it made you miss or maybe not miss home? For example, what does "home" mean to you now that you have experienced living at MSU?

Student A: That's a good question, and to be honest, I have thought about it a lot. For me, home means family. That's where my heart is. I mean, I get it that home is all fucked up cause it's the ghetto; but it is still home for me, and I love it.

Teacher: Okay, so are you saying that home means family to you?

Student A: Yes.

Teacher: Anyone else willing to share their thoughts on this?

Student B: I never thought of home in the past because I was there every day and had never left. Now that I have finally left, I see things differently. All of the stuff that happens back home has been negative for me. So for me, home means a place I don't want to go back to; and if I can, I want to stay here at MSU.

Teacher: So tell us in one word or a few what home means to you.

Student B: It means drama that I don't need or want.

Teacher: Okay, so home in this case means drama. One more person want to share?

Student C: Home for me is where all of my experiences have happened. Like good ones and bad ones. So coming here, I know I am willing to leave home for a while so I can get my education, but I want to go back.

Teacher: Why do you want to go back?

Student C: 'Cause to me home is my heart. It's what made me the way I am today; and I ain't fucking perfect, but I'm a good person who has been through a lot of stuff. I know people judge us when we come from the hood in all kinds of negative ways, but for real, I'm not ashamed of where I am from.

Teacher: So home represents your heart?

Student C: Yes.

Teacher: Okay, as you can all see and have already thought about for yourselves, home means something very powerful for all of us, sometimes in similar ways and very different other times. Like for me, home was the only place I knew growing up, and I just accepted what it was. But when I went away and started seeing and experiencing new things, I would think back to home, and I would become really angry. I would think back to home, and I was angry at all the deep poverty and inequality that I went through and that exists where I came from. So home was a painful memory. But eventually, I got to a place where home was where my heart will always be, and I embraced and appreciated everything I learned, both good and bad, because it allowed me to become who I am today. It gave me strength and insight that I would not have gotten anywhere else, and now home is a place that gives me strength wherever I am in the world. I ain't trippin' that I no longer live back home because home exists in my heart, and it symbolizes my strength when I feel weak. Does this make sense to everyone?

Various Students: Yes. Yeah, I feel you. Yup.

Teacher: Okay, what we just did was use symbolism within our own lives. You see, we all have something that reminds us of something else—whether it is home and what it symbolizes to us or when you think of what America symbolizes to each of you, what police departments symbolize for us, or how when you think of a certain type of animal it may represent power or agility or speed or the like to us. The point is that symbolism is a part of our everyday lives, and we all use it in similar and, at times, very different ways. We have to use what you just did with me in a way now that focuses these same ideas on figuring out how the GED uses symbolism in some of the questions you will be asked on the exam. So I need your help in being open to trying to learn about symbolism from the standpoint of what you are going to be learning from your books today. So—you all ready to get cracking on the symbolism section?

Various Students: Yeah, let's do it. I'm with it. A'ight.

Appendix F

"Who I Am" Real Talk on the First Day of Class

This is the Real Talk I used with my students on the first day of class. It is an excellent way to show students that you are a real person, not an adversary—that your position as teacher is only one facet of who you are. Using this Real Talk will help you set the tone for the way you will conduct class.

Teacher: Good morning, class. My name is Dr. Paul Hernandez, and I want not only to welcome you but, if you give me the chance, to share a little bit about myself and how and why I teach in the manner I do. Let me show you who I am as a person before you decide that I am simply a teacher.

[Students are staring at me with looks of bewilderment, curiosity, and, in some cases, defensiveness.]

Teacher: Standing in front of you is a former dropout and someone who not only struggled in school but hated everything about it. I remember many different occasions when I was told that I was dumb or that I was better off just going to work instead of being in school. I was treated more like a "thing" rather than a person. It was a punishment for me to have to go to school, but ultimately, it was not because I was stupid or because I was lazy. There were many other things going on in my life that affected my ability to put school as number one in my life. Combining my life with being treated disrespectfully by some educators pushed me to eventually walk away from school.

[Students perk up and listen more intently as they focus on what I am sharing.]

Teacher: It was all of the harsh challenges I faced from growing up in deep poverty with my momma, who was a single mother; the road blocks that were put in front of me by haters who wanted to see me fail; or the fact that I was raised within the gang culture of Los Angeles—all played a role in why I stand in front of you here today.

[Students are captivated by what is being said. They say nothing, but their attention is directed at me. You can hear a pin drop in the classroom. A few are still showing resistance with their body language but are focusing on what I am saying.]

Teacher: This class and what I have to offer is all about you and finding a way to have you pass the sections of the GED we are preparing to take. But we will not just focus on our book; we will incorporate the real world and our experiences into this class.

For me, it's an honor to have the opportunity to work with you; and with your help, I know we can turn this class into something positive and different than any other class you have ever had. If you give me the opportunity, not only will we learn how to pass the GED, but we will also grow in order to get ready to succeed beyond the GED.

You will get to know me and I will get to know you; but I want you to see the real me, and I hope you let me see the real you as it will help us in making sure we work well together as we move forward. For me, it was my education that ultimately helped me reach heights that I never imagined, and even as I stand here in front of you, I can't even believe I made it out of the situations I faced throughout my life. Now, do you have any questions before we get started with the work we have to start chipping away at?

Various Students: Damn, that's some real shit.

Did you ever meet your dad? I already like this class.

I ain't ever had a teacher talk to me the way you just did.

How old are you?

Is your mom proud of you?

Appendix G

Real Talk on Adversity

The teacher is in front of the room as students enter the class. Informal conversation takes place between the students and teacher as students settle in and prepare for the class.

Teacher: Class, may I have your attention? How is everyone doing today? How are you doing today, Jay? How was last night? You feeling all right?

Student A: I'm all right. I'm feeling a little tired because I didn't sleep much last night. But it's all good because I was studying, and I am ready for Round 2 today.

Teacher: Good! I'm glad you are studying! If you have any specific questions, just holler at me. But try to find a balance because I want you to feel rested because I want you to keep learning. This goes for all of you. Work hard but find a balance so you feel rested and ready to work every day.

[Students are starting to listen intently; a few students are raising their hands to respond to the initial question.]

Teacher: Big T, what do you wanna share?

Student B: It's hard to find a balance. Sometimes I wanna work all night, and sometimes I don't wanna do shit.

Teacher: That's a great point. I feel like that sometimes myself. Does anyone else feel like it's difficult to find a balance sometimes?

Various Students:	Yeah.
	Shit's hard.
	It's a struggle.
	For sure.
	Yeah, sometimes life ain't easy.
Teacher:	You see, the thing we are talking about right now is dealing with adversity. Adversity means hard times, and we all go through hard times in this world. Regardless of where we come from, everyone struggles in their own way at some point in their lives to make it through a day, a week, a month, a year. For me, adversity has meant so many different things.
	Adversity when I was a kid meant having a single mother who worked as hard as she could yet we had nothing. My momma was forced to work seven days a week and 15 hours day; so as much as she tried to be there for us, she struggled to find a balance. I remember as a little boy the daily struggles were not knowing if we would have anything to eat, a place to live, and if we would even survive to see the next day. Even though I had my brothers and my momma, I felt isolated and alone, living in a world that did not care if I would live or die. That was the type of adversity I dealt with as a kid, and I always felt that no one understood what I was going through. When I went to community college, adversity meant something else. I had to learn and teach myself how to pay attention, take notes, and even care about passing a class. Just trying to focus, forcing myself to go to class after a whole 12-hour shift of work was a struggle. I mean, it was so much easier to just give up, throw in the towel, walk away, and put in overtime to make a few extra bucks. Trying to go to school, succeed in school, and make a dream come true was a daily challenge. I had no one to help me but myself. You feel me? You understand what I am telling you?
Various Students:	Yeah, I feel you.
	You are right; it's a struggle.
	I can't believe you had to go through that. Yeah, man, it has been tough.

Teacher: You see, I could tell you stories about my struggles all day, but the point of this is to figure out what struggles you go through so we can figure out how to beat them and succeed in the class. This ain't about me; it's about you. What's standing in your way to make this GED come true? What stood in your way in the past that makes you think or worry that you can't make it to college? 'Cause I am here to tell you that we are going to make this thing happen.

Student C: It's always been hard having so many people in the family and everyone being broke. It's hard to focus 'cause you just wanna help your family. You wanna go work and bring money home to make sure everyone can eat. This is the type of thing that was always riding my mind when I tried the school thing. I ain't gonna lie; I think about this all the time. That's why it's so hard being here.

Teacher: Trust me when I say we all feel you. You are not the only one in this room who feels an obligation to his family. But what you just shared is the type of thing I need you all to be open about so we can figure out what doesn't allow us to focus on the work at hand.

Student D: Yeah, it's hard 'cause I think of my kids. And I want to be there and support them, but I know I gotta be here to get my GED.

Student E: I'm worried that I'm out here trying this shit, and all my people are proud of me but I'm not gonna make it. I ain't scared of shit, but I don't wanna let everybody down.

Teacher: That's it! You see, every single one of us in here has these daily challenges. Our biggest challenge sitting here in this class is preparing to pass this GED. Everything you guys have talked about we can improve by improving ourselves by passing and getting the GED. Getting the GED will be the manner in which we overcome adversity this semester. Getting the GED will open up new doors for us. These new doors will allow you to better yourself with jobs, more schooling that can help with your families back home. As a class, in my class, together we will overcome the adversity we face in the

GED. Now, you feeling me? You see me? This is the kind of thing I wanna discuss in class in order to keep us motivated and focused on passing the GED. It will not be easy at times, but we will overcome the adversity we face with preparing to pass the GED together.

What we are going to do now is take these thoughts on adversity, these things you shared with me, and write them down. We must practice the fundamental writing techniques that will support your GED writing as we discussed yesterday in Lesson 8 and Lesson 10 regarding a strong topic sentence in your essay, clear transition sentences, and phrases. So let's turn to these sections in your books and get ready to get some work done.

NOTES

Appendix H

Real Talk on Individuality in Learning

For this Real Talk, SP focused on individuality in learning. She felt strongly about diverse learners in the classroom. Real Talk's structure and intentionality gave her a method to connect with her students and help them with their learning. Although I am providing her written example, she conducted this Real Talk by recording herself and posting it for her class to watch. SP's written Real Talk follows.

Have you ever felt trapped by the requirements of formalized education—meaning, have you ever felt your learning has been stifled by the specifications of the work assigned to you? Consider how that's affected your interest and persistence in continued education.

I was not initially interested in attending college at all. While I've always been a good student on paper, I never enjoyed being in school because I felt constrained by the type of learning that was demanded of me. Traditional education formats—sitting in a room, listening to lectures, memorizing information for exams—were just not something I wanted to do more of. Eventually, I decided to go to college anyway, and I started off with my old habits: checking to see how many absences I could get away with, seeing what days I would need to cram for exams, learning what my teachers wanted me to memorize so I could spit it back out to them. However, as I got into my major-specific classes (film and video production), I was much more interested and engaged because of the ability to be creative and kinesthetic in my learning. As a result, I did better in those classes and became more excited about attending classes. I want to offer that same opportunity to each of you.

For structure's sake, there is a traditional three-to-five-page research paper assignment for your final in this class. *However,* I want you to keep an open mind when reviewing it and reach out to me if nothing fits your interests as they pertain to this class. If you would prefer to explore another option that would be more beneficial to your future and would enhance your learning, propose it to me, and we will work to create an assignment that is a better fit for your interests and learning style. As you've seen throughout this class, I've tried very hard to keep things interesting and engaging and personal, so I want that to continue on through the final.

Do you express your learning better in video or audio than you do in writing? Let's talk about what you can submit in lieu of a paper! Did none of the chapters specifically address your interest in the field of media? Let's talk about how we can adapt one or two of them into something specific to your goals! Are you undecided on which aspect of media you want to pursue? Let's develop a final that allows you to explore a few! You can pitch me a final project if what I have assigned is not suited to your goals and/or learning style. I look forward to seeing what you come up with!

NOTES

Appendix I

Real Talk on Being Authentic

This particular Real Talk was created by an art teacher who had been teaching for over 25 years and initially struggled to grasp Real Talk.

Her passion toward seeing her students succeed drove her to work hard to empower them. She was willing to learn something new and eventually created a Real Talk to try in her art lab. In this class, a majority of her students typically displayed feelings of trepidation. It was a challenge to get her students to let their defenses down to do art. She decided a Real Talk might be effective in doing so.

She began her Real Talk by sharing with her class an experience from college that had left an unforgettable impact on her as an artist and as a woman. Mr. M was one of her instructors who taught her, as a young college art student, about being authentic. Mr. M was terminally ill with cancer. His wife had also passed away, and he was raising his young children. In addition to all this, he was a paraplegic. She described him to the class as a man who had to use his upper-body strength to propel his entire body, using crutches and dragging his legs to walk.

After describing the man, she explained that his doctors had strongly encouraged him to take numbing drugs (tranquilizers) to ease his physical and emotional pain. Mr. M had refused to do so because, as an artist, he wanted to feel all of the emotions he carried. This teacher had felt bad for him because she could see how he loved so deeply. The love that Mr. M had for his wife had allowed him to feel both the positive emotions of having been with her and the painful emotions of having lost her. Mr. M had said that, as an artist, he would not deny himself the experience of any of his emotions, especially the painful ones, explaining that without feeling the pain he could never illustrate it in his art. To her, Mr. M was larger than life, one of the most authentic people she had ever met.

She told them that throughout her life the experience and message Mr. M conveyed gave her courage—the courage and inspiration to be authentic. She shared some brief experiences about being authentic: homeschooling her children, home birthing, and traveling around the world. These personal experiences were resources for her art and writing. She elaborated that, like a ripple in a pond, Mr. M continued to be her teacher. She then explained that she had allowed her students a peek into her journey as an artist so they could see that an artist must be willing to be courageous and authentic for their art to be successful. Lastly, she explained that, in her art class, students should try to be in touch with themselves and reality. In this way, their artwork would be explosive, powerful, and compelling. She concluded her Real Talk by sharing that authenticity means accepting yourself, knowing yourself, and having the courage to illustrate your truth.

The teacher told us that throughout the entire Real Talk, including a few seconds after she was done, the classroom was enveloped in a profound silence because the students were very quiet and listening intently. This type of attention was not a norm in her class. After the silence, students began to ask her questions about Mr. M, and several students began to share their own experiences. One young woman in her class shared how her uncle was as an inspiration to her because he battled and eventually overcame his addiction. The teacher was surprised that several students said goodbye to her after class and told her to have a nice day. This type of gesture was also not customary of her students. Another outcome of the Real Talk was that a young male student came to see the teacher during lunch to share his own personal story. The final outcome, she noted, occurred the next day in class: All her students greeted her, and they began to work with their art directly. This went on for several days—again, not the type of behavior that was common for her students in the art lab.

Appendix J

Real Talk on Classroom Norms

This English teacher decided to use her first Real Talk on the first day of her class. After a training session, this teacher spoke to me about an idea for a Real Talk on drug use. She was nervous and not sure how to approach this issue. She had a great idea but needed a boost in her confidence and reassurance; she also needed someone to help her get the details straight for her delivery. Together, we solidified the approach for Real Talk. On the first day of class, this teacher announced her classroom rules, specifically highlighting one rule that upset her students: Laying their heads down or sleeping/nodding off was not permitted in her class. She detailed that any student doing so would get a written referral. As always, when she shared this information with her students, they responded with resistance, complaining and speaking under their breath.

The difference this time was that she had created a Real Talk to use at this point in the class. She began by sharing with them an experience she had had in one of her classrooms that led to her creating this rule. Students were curious and began to listen as they realized that the rationale was directly connected to her experience with other students. A few years ago, the police had brought police dogs to search the school for drugs. She elaborately explained how chaotic everything was as the dogs searched and eventually found the drugs in her classroom. As she stood there listening to the dog barking excessively, she knew it had done its job. Her students at that time had sat calmly while the dog barked directly at one student. This experience had really shaken her up.

She then told her current students that her job was to help them succeed in school and to achieve their educational goals for the betterment of their lives. She couldn't compete with drugs in the classroom. She explained that teaching was not a backup job for her; it was her chosen career. She had gone to school for six years and had invested large amounts of her personal money to further her education to serve her students better. Her goal was ultimately to see her students graduate from high school and succeed with their lives. She could not reach those goals when her students chose drugs over school.

Rather than end the Real Talk, she moved to the next component, sharing another experience in her classroom that had happened within the past few years. She had a student who seemed to be sleepy or drowsy one afternoon and put his head down to sleep. She told the student several times not to do so and finally removed the student from class. When the student was taken to the administrator's office, the truth was discovered: He was having a very negative effect from the heroin he had taken earlier that day. Her removing him from class had helped ensure he did not die from the drugs as two other students had done previously at the school. These experiences had pushed her to the edge, causing her to question her career, because they had hit her very hard and weighed heavily on her. After a few days, she came to the realization as a person and as a teacher that her position was to make sure she did everything possible to affect her students positively, helping them to make the best choices they could to be successful and responsible.

She ended the Real Talk by connecting it back to norms in her classroom. Her experiences with her former students and many other personal experiences were the reasons behind the rules in her class, including the one about not laying their heads down in class. These rules were created to help and benefit her students. After she concluded, her students asked many sincere questions about the experiences she had shared.

After her Real Talk, the class atmosphere was positive, something she had rarely encountered after going over classroom rules. Several weeks later, the teacher further reflected on this specific Real Talk. She noted that this was the best class she had ever had regarding students putting their heads down in her class. It was hardly an issue at all, and she no longer had to have discussions with her students about why they couldn't sleep in her class. She felt strongly that the Real Talk helped her students see her perspective on this particular issue. She wasn't just a grouchy teacher who was giving them a hard time. She also felt far more connected to this class than she had with previous classes in her many years of teaching.

Appendix K

Examples of Real Talk Themes

In order to show the diversity and breadth of themes teachers have used to create Real Talks, I am including the following table. The choices for themes are practically endless. Selecting a theme sometimes serves as a daunting obstacle for teachers. With what I have provided throughout the book and additionally here, I hope to make choosing a theme easily tangible.

Happiness	Powerfulness	Frustration	Triumph	Fear
Humor	Commitment	Motivation	Powerlessness	Clarity
Comfort	Courage	Kindness	Support	Loyalty
Excitement	Encouragement	Endurance	Alertness	Honesty
Hopefulness	Hopelessness	Passion	Sacrifice	Trust

NOTES

Appendix L

Bridge Project Packet

Name: _____ Hour: _____

Mini Lesson 1:
Center of Mass and Gravity

Gravity is: _____

_____

_____

_____

_____

_____

_____

Center of mass is: _____

_____

_____

_____

_____

_____

_____

Finding Center of Mass

When I stand straight up, my center of mass is . . .

When I stand on my left foot, my center of mass is . . .

When I lean against a wall with the left part of my body, my center of mass is . . .

Image source: https://www.istockphoto.com/portfolio/MaskaRad

Stability is: _____
_____
_____

The _____ a building is, the _____ the base must be because:
_____
_____

Draw a building that would be stable and a building that would not be stable, and then write one sentence for each to explain why:

Stable Building	Not Stable Building
Explanation: _____ _____ _____ _____	Explanation: _____ _____ _____ _____

To ensure the _____ amount of weight is held by the bridge, where should the weight be placed? _____

If the weight is not placed in the middle, what will happen? (Use two vocabulary words that we learned today and give two sentences.)

_____
_____
_____
_____

Explain how you will use what we learned today to make the best bridge.

_____
_____
_____
_____

Draw a sample bridge and show where the center of mass will be.

Mini Lesson 2: Symmetry And Power of the Triangle

Draw three images you created on http://www.mathsisfun.com/geometry/symmetry-artist.html.

$y = x$ axis	origin	x axis

Symmetry is: _____
_____
_____.

Give four reasons why symmetry is important in structures.

1. _____
2. _____
3. _____
4. _____

Our bridges must be symmetric _____ and
_____.

Why is symmetry important to the design of our bridges? _____
_____
_____
_____

Draw a sketch of a bridge that is symmetric and one that is not.

Symmetric Bridge Design	Non-Symmetric Bridge Design

Triangles

Prediction: I think the strongest shape to use in a bridge is _____. I think this because _____ _____. A _____ is the strongest structural shape there is. This is because _____

_____

_____

_____.

Creating Shapes

Draw three shapes you created with the cardstock and fasteners. Circle the weak points in the structure.

Redraw the shape you made after you made it stronger with triangles.

Shape 1	Shape 2	Shape 3
Shape 1 With Triangles	**Shape 2 With Triangles**	**Shape 3 With Triangles**

Why are your shapes stronger now that you have added triangles? How do you know they are stronger?

_____

_____

_____

How can you incorporate triangles into your bridge design?

_____

_____

Design of the Bridge

Before you start building your bridge, you must sketch a draft of what you hope your bridge will look like. Remember the bridge must span a distance of 40 cm. Try measuring the width of a Popsicle stick and determine how many you will need for the base of the bridge.

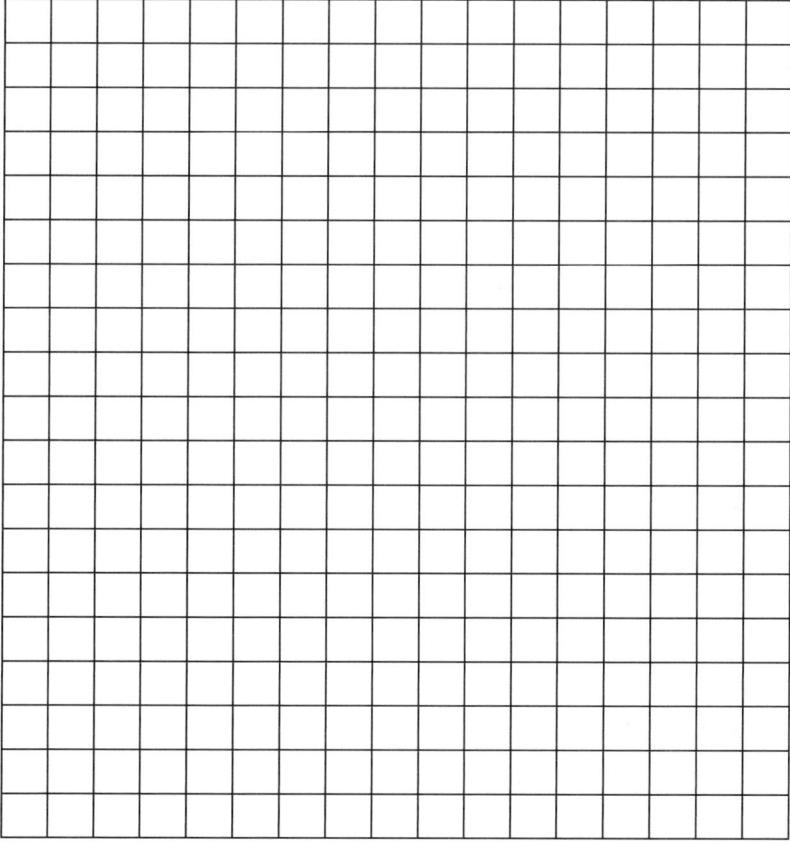

Formal College Experiment Report

Objective: _____

_____

_____

_____

_____

_____

_____

_____

_____

Materials:

_____

Hypothesis: _____

_____

_____

_____

_____

_____

_____

_____

Procedure:

_____

_____

_____

_____

_____

_____

_____

Calculations

One Popsicle stick is _____ wide and _____ long. I need _____ Popsicle sticks to make sure my bridge is long enough. These are shapes I will use in my bridge and how I will use them:

Graphs

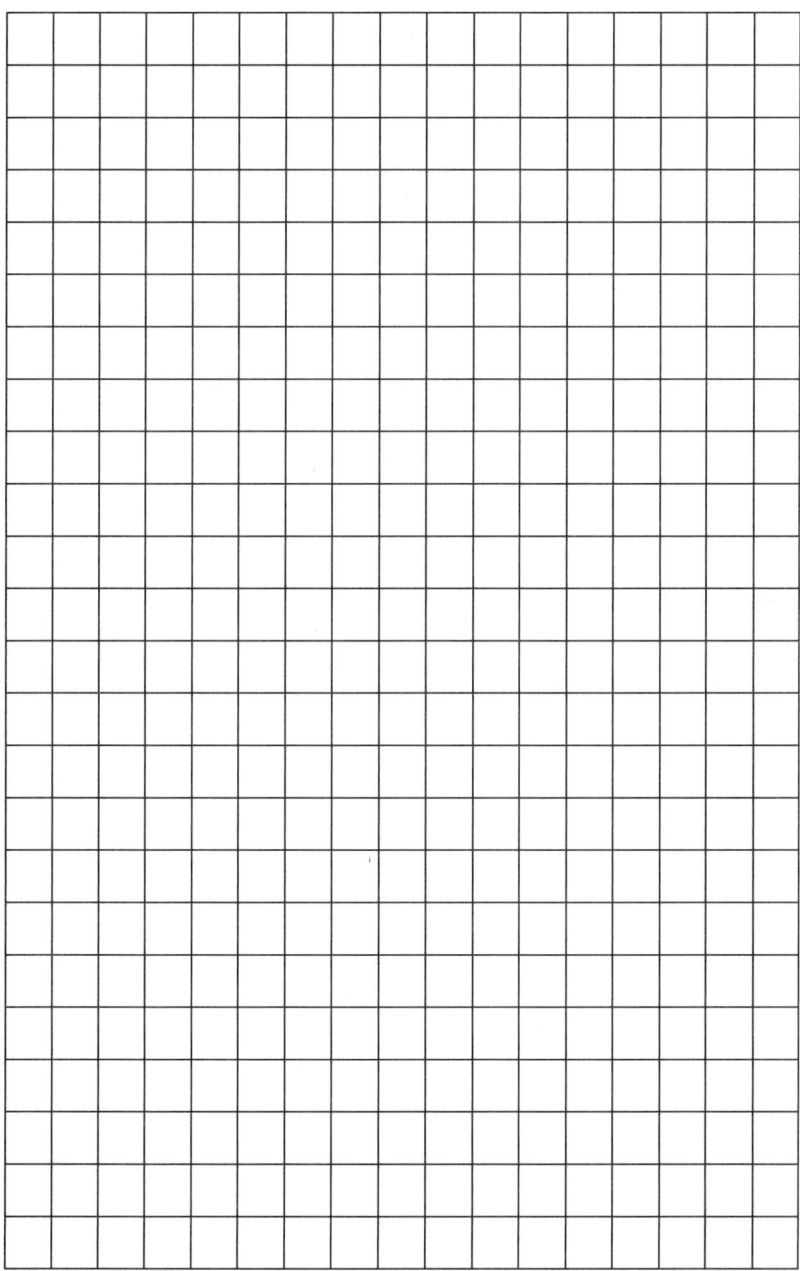

Analysis:

_____

_____

_____

_____

_____

_____

Conclusion:

_____

_____

_____

_____

_____

_____

My hypothesis was _____

_____

because _____

_____ .

Revision and Reflection:

Every good scientist and mathematician looks back on his or her design critically and thinks about how the design could be better.

Our challenge:

In this class, we have so many brilliant brains, so if we put them together, could we as a class come up with an even better bridge that can withstand 100 pounds?

What do we need to do?

_____

Peer-to-Peer Evaluation

GROUP	PICTURE	I THINK THIS BRIDGE WILL HOLD BECAUSE . . . (MINIMUM ONE SENTENCE)	THIS BRIDGE IS GOOD BECAUSE . . . (MINIMUM ONE SENTENCE)	RATING 1—10 (1 LOWEST, 10 HIGHEST)

Appendix M

Alternative Lesson on Congruent Triangles

This lesson was created by the math teacher I spoke of in Chapter 11, "Training and Feedback." This is an excellent example of a clear difference between a Real Talk (see Appendix D) and an alternative lesson. The Real Talk and alternative lesson both focused on congruent triangles and assumptions but were used according to how each is defined and meant to be used in the classroom.

The alternative lesson she created focused on the highly publicized murder case of Casey Anthony. Even though this case was very popular around the country, the teacher did not assume that all her students knew about the case and, thus, introduced the case as the starting point of the alternative lesson. She purposely selected the following story because she knew it would strike a chord or resonate with her class, given the information she had learned about their terministic screens. She introduced the case by showing a YouTube clip that summarized the murder trial. Occasionally, instead of showing the video, she would hand out a one-page article highlighting the case and would elaborate on the details of the story.

The Casey Anthony murder trial was highly controversial around the country. Casey Anthony was accused of murdering her two-year-old daughter, Caylee (Alvarez, 2011). Despite the enormous amount of evidence and the numerous expert witnesses testifying in the attempt to convict Casey Anthony of murdering her daughter, that was not the outcome. The media coverage for this case was massive and widespread, with many people within the media and public sector having very strong opinions on the matter of Casey Anthony's guilt. When Casey

Anthony was acquitted by the jury, the media and country erupted with outcries that she was getting away with murder. By the end of the introduction of the murder trial, all of the students were familiar with the details of the story and were asked about their opinions on the case.

The teacher highlighted the public opinion component of how an overwhelming majority of the public considered her guilty. She followed this by asking students for their opinions on the matter. Many students shared their perspectives and thoughts on the case and eventually the teacher asked the class, "Why was Casey Anthony acquitted despite public opinion?" Students were captivated by the story; it connected with them, making them not only receptive but also willing to participate. Students began to answer. The teacher eventually stepped in to tie things directly to the lesson she had for the students. She shared that although there was evidence against Casey Anthony the case illustrated the importance of having the right evidence. She then introduced congruent triangles and the appropriate information to answer questions correctly. She transitioned by explaining that having the correct evidence is a crucial component in proving that two triangles are congruent. She explained that it does not matter if the two triangles look the same (heck, maybe they are the same!); if that information isn't given or if the right pieces of information aren't given, no one can prove that the two triangles are congruent. She followed this by handing out the following assignment.

Congruent Triangles Investigation

Name: _____

You are a lawyer at an important math law firm that helps prove whether or not two triangles are congruent. Remember, in order for two triangles to be congruent, all of their corresponding sides must be congruent and all of their corresponding angles must be congruent! There are a few shortcuts you can use to prove that two triangles are congruent. You can win the trial if you can prove that one of the five following triangle congruencies apply to your case:

SSS: _____

SAS: _____

AAS: _____

ASA: _____

RHL: _____

You may need to collect additional evidence in order to win your case. For each piece of additional evidence you collect, you must be able to back it up in court with a valid mathematical justification. A list of common theorems and properties is attached at the end of this packet.

Case 1: Lindsey and Kenzie were both adopted as young triangles. Twenty years later, they met at a party and their resemblance couldn't be denied! After a long discussion, they came to the conclusion that they must be identical twins. Since genetic testing isn't available for triangles, they have come to you to help them prove that they are congruent triangles.

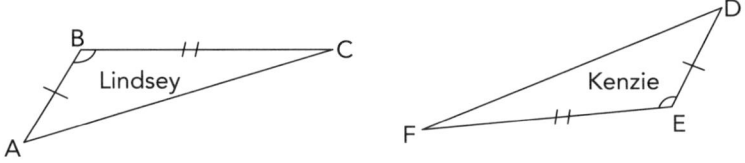

Facts: What information is given to you (either in a given statement or information from the diagrams)?

Evidence: What information, if any, do you still need to gather? How can you prove that this new information is true?

Your Conclusion: What is your conclusion (are the two triangles congruent)? What triangle congruency did you use to make your claim?

Case 2: A local storeowner has come to you needing legal representation. One night, his store was robbed. Security cameras recorded the robbery and, based on the footage, a local triangle named Jeff is being accused of the robbery. Jeff claims it can't be him because only some of his features are the same as in the security footage. The storeowner wants you to prove that Jeff is guilty of committing the robbery by proving that Jeff is the same triangle that was captured in the security footage.

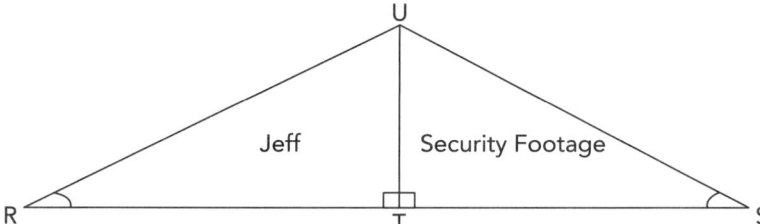

Jeff agrees that his angle R is the same as the angle S in the footage and that both he and the triangle in the footage have the same angle T. However, Jeff claims that you can't provide enough additional evidence to prove he is the same triangle in the footage.

Facts: What information is given to you (either in a given statement or information from the diagrams)?

Evidence: What information, if any, do you still need to gather? How can you prove that this new information is true?

Your Conclusion: What is your conclusion (are the two triangles congruent)? What triangle congruency did you use to make your claim?

The judge has asked that you present your evidence in the form of a two-column proof. Fill in the two-column proof below:

EVIDENCE	JUSTIFICATION
1.	1.
2.	2.
3.	3.

Case 3: Maria is being accused of a crime she claims she didn't commit. A house in her neighborhood was broken into a few nights ago, and a neighbor claimed that she saw Maria sneaking around the backyard. However, Maria has photos of herself at a party that were taken at the same time that the breaking and entering occurred. The neighbor does not believe Maria's alibi and does not think that the triangle in the pictures is Maria. Maria has come to you to help her clear her name and prove that she is the same triangle that is in the picture.

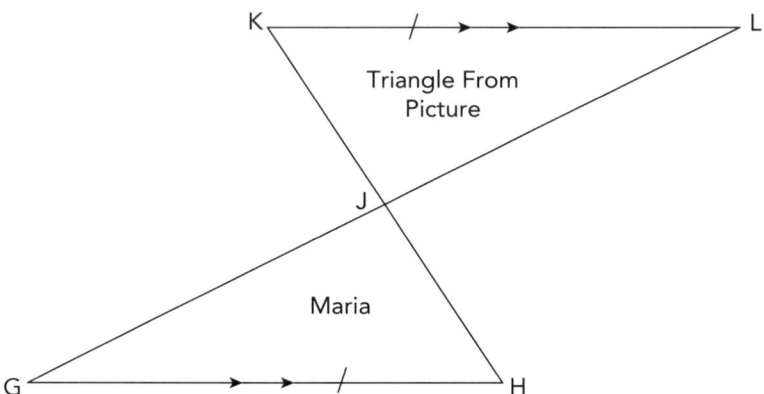

The only information that Maria can give you is that her side $\overline{GH}$ is parallel and congruent to the side $\overline{LK}$ in the picture.

Facts: What information is given to you (either in a given statement or information from the diagrams)?

Evidence: What information, if any, do you still need to gather? How can you prove that this new information is true?

Your Conclusion: What is your conclusion (are the two triangles congruent)? What triangle congruency did you use to make your claim?

Important Theorems and Properties: Use These for Proofs

Vertical Angles

All vertical angles are congruent

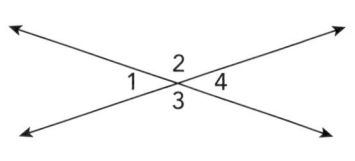

∠1 ≅ ∠4 and ∠2 ≅ ∠3

Alternate Interior Angles

If two parallel lines are cut by a transversal, then the pairs of alternate interior angles are congruent.

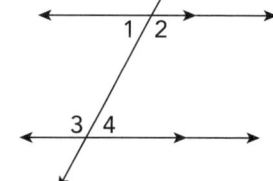

∠1 ≅ ∠4 and ∠2 ≅ ∠3

Triangle Sum Theorem

The sum of the measure of the interior angles of a triangle is 180°.

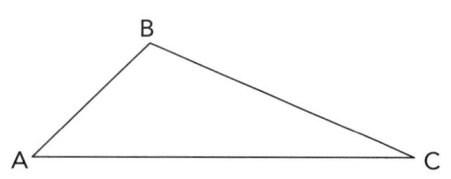

$m\angle A + m\angle B + m\angle C = 180°$

Corresponding Angles

If two parallel lines are cut by a transversal, then the pairs of corresponding angles are congruent.

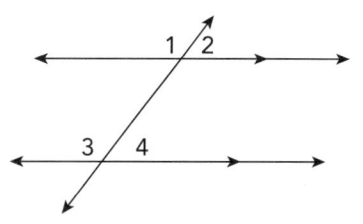

∠1 ≅ ∠3 and ∠2 ≅ ∠4

(Continued)

(Continued)

Reflexive Property of Congruence

Any side or angle is congruent to itself.

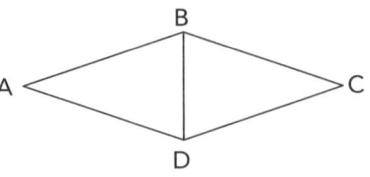

$\overline{BD} \cong \overline{BD}$

Third Angle Theorem

If two angles of one triangle are congruent to two angles of another triangle, then the third angles are also congruent.

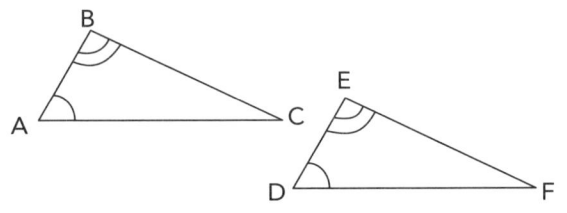

If $\angle A \cong \angle D$ and $\angle B \cong \angle E$, then $\angle C \cong \angle F$

Appendix N

Alternative Lesson on Graphing Different Types of Linear Systems

For this alternative lesson, I have used another math example. This teacher created a wonderful alternative lesson based on Bernie Madoff. The teacher had approached me after a professional development day with her school and asked if I could help her with topics that would connect to her students. I decided to help her brainstorm, first focusing on her students and what she had learned about them through Real Talk. She mentioned a variety of things, but the thing that jumped out at me the most was their issues with money. She mentioned that her students had strong connections to money: not having any, not having enough, wanting as much as possible, ways to achieve monetary success, and so forth.

With this in mind, I proposed that the teacher use Bernie Madoff as the topic for her lesson. The case was a high-profile and well-publicized case. It was also a very intimate topic based on the crimes committed by Madoff. I suggested she use the angle of the Ponzi scheme that Madoff used to steal $50 billion from people. She was familiar with the case and knew her class far better than I did and felt that my suggestion would work well with her students. Based on our conversation, she created the alternative lesson based on the Bernie Madoff Ponzi scheme.

In her alternative lesson, she first introduced Bernie Madoff and what he did to his investors. She did not assume all of her students knew the story or knew who he was, so she showed the class a YouTube clip (CBS News, 2008). The video was less than five minutes in length. It summarized Bernie Madoff's crime, gave a short explanation of the Ponzi scheme he used to rob his investors, identified the people and companies his crime affected, and included an interview with an elderly couple who lost their entire life savings because of Madoff. After showing the video, she elaborated on what a Ponzi scheme is to make sure that it was clear to her students. She phrased what Madoff did as a "hustle" to rob innocent investors. To connect it directly to her students, as she ended her explanation of the Madoff Ponzi scheme, she asked her students, "How would you feel if you lost everything after an entire life of hard work?" Her students were eager to participate, and many of them answered her question with well-thought-out and profound answers because they could empathize with the victims. Some students even had their own stories of friends or family who had lost their savings or large amounts of money.

Once she felt comfortable with the class participation and with allowing her students to openly share their terministic screens, she transitioned into handing out the following assignment. Later she shared that throughout the entire video and her lecture, her students were entirely engaged. She also shared her excitement with me about being able to create such an effective alternative lesson.

Types of Systems of Equations

Name: _____

Problem 1: Bernie Madoff is scamming money from two people, and he wants to know from which one of them he will earn the most over time:

Bob makes an initial investment of $100 and pays Madoff an additional $300 each month.

Equation: _____

Matt makes an initial investment of $1,000 and pays an additional $150 each month.

Equation: _____

Graph the two equations on the grid below and create a table of values. You may use your graphing calculator for assistance. Use a different color to graph the lines for Bob and Matt.

*HINT: Adjust your window! x range from 0–10 with an x-scl of 1. y range from 0–5000 with a y-scl of 500.

BOB			MATT	
X MONTHS	Y PROFIT		X MONTHS	Y PROFIT
0			0	
1			1	
2			2	
3			3	
4			4	
5			5	
6			6	
7			7	
8			8	
9			9	
10			10	

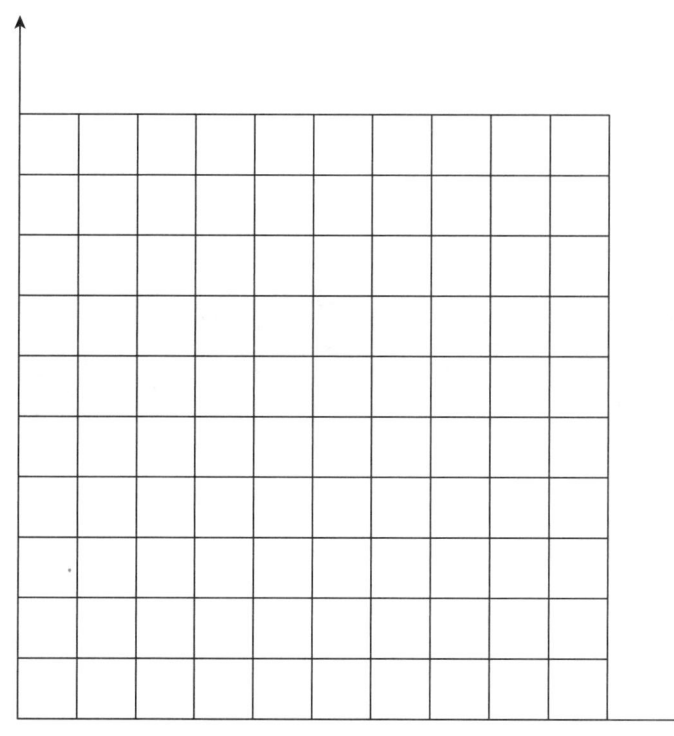

Who is more profitable after two months? _____

Who is more profitable after eight months? _____

At what point will Bob and Matt be equally profitable? _____

Madoff can choose either Bob or Matt to collect money from for one year. Madoff wants to earn as much money as possible. Whom should he choose and why? _____

_____

Problem 2: Bernie Madoff has two more people willing to give him money. Each gives him the same amount of money per month, but he collects different start-up fees from each person:

Pearl makes an initial investment of $100 and pays Madoff an additional $300 each month.

Equation:_____

Felicia makes an initial investment of $500 and pays an additional $300 each month.

Equation: _____

Graph the two equations on the grid below and create a table of values. You may use your graphing calculator for assistance. Use a different color to graph the lines for Pearl and Felicia.

*HINT: Adjust your window! x range from 0–10 with an x-scl of 1. y range from 0–5000 with a y-scl of 500.

PEARL			FELICIA	
X MONTHS	Y PROFIT		X MONTHS	Y PROFIT
0			0	
1			1	
2			2	
3			3	
4			4	
5			5	

PEARL			FELICIA	
X MONTHS	Y PROFIT		X MONTHS	Y PROFIT
6			6	
7			7	
8			8	
9			9	
10			10	

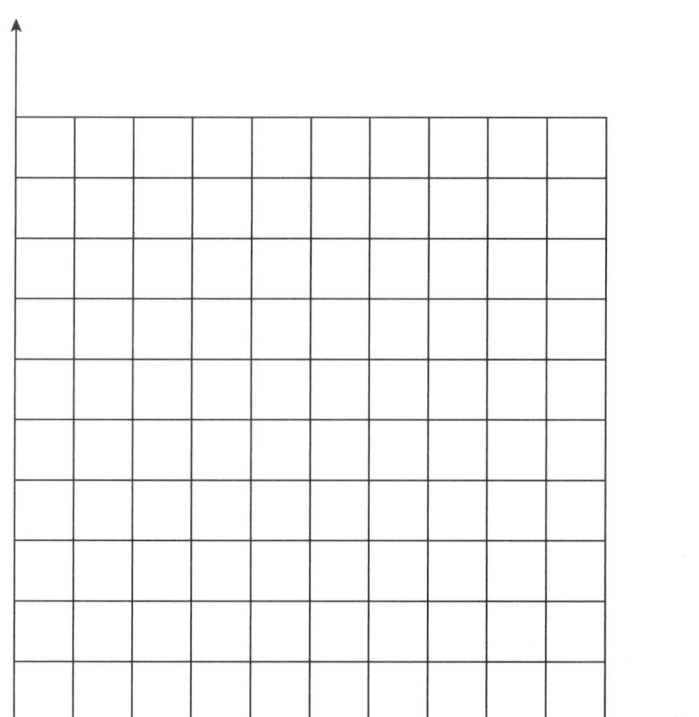

Who is more profitable after two months? _____

Who is more profitable after eight months? _____

Will Pearl ever be more profitable than Felicia? Why or why not?
_____
_____

Problem 3: Jake and Deshawn are eager to pool their money and make an investment with Madoff. Madoff has offered them two choices:

Choice A: Madoff will collect a total of $300 from Jake and Deshawn, with Jake paying in increments of $75 (i.e., $75, $150, $225 . . .) and Deshawn paying in increments of $50.

Equation: _____

Choice B: Madoff will collect a total of $600 from Jake and Deshawn, with Jake paying in increments of $150 and Deshawn paying in increments of $100.

Equation: _____

Graph the two equations. Use a different color for Choice A and Choice B.

*HINT!: Graph by finding the x and y intercepts for each equation!

What are three different combinations of money Jake and Deshawn could pay for Choice A?

_____

_____

_____

_____

_____

What are three different combinations of money Jake and Deshawn could pay for Choice B?

_____

_____

_____

_____

_____

Let x be the number of increments that Jake contributes and y be the increments that Deshawn contributes. Is there a combination of increments that would be a possible solution for Choice A yet would *not* work for Choice B? Explain:

_____

_____

_____

_____

_____

Copyright © 2022 by Corwin. All rights reserved. Reprinted from *The Pedagogy of Real Talk: Engaging, Teaching, and Connecting With Students At-Promise* by Paul Hernandez. Thousand Oaks, CA: Corwin, www.corwin.com.

Appendix O

Alternative Lesson on Public Speaking Anxiety

In this lesson, a teacher who teaches technology, English, and public speaking (speech) classes was attempting to create a lesson to help his public speaking students. The students in his class were typically anxious when it came to public speaking. This led many of them to act out in a variety of ways and not to take the work in class seriously or even to put forth any effort in the class. After conducting a Real Talk during the first week of class, he followed this by introducing an alternative lesson that same week. The alternative lesson was very creative, using zombies to address public speaking anxiety. The teacher's objectives in this alternative lesson were to create open communication with individual students and between the students and the teacher, as well as to introduce the uncomfortable subject of anxiety. In using this introductory alternative lesson, he was also attempting to overcome the traditional resistance he encountered with his students when beginning this class. The outcome he desired for himself and his students was to give his students a way to examine their anxiety about the course to allow them to begin working toward creating and executing speeches in the class. He wanted his students to begin the class on a positive note by using a lesson that shows the issue of anxiety connected to public speaking as a normal process in this particular class. Thus, he set the tone for the class in the first lesson: knowing and accepting that if they feel any anxiety with public speaking, they must address it before they can move forward in the class.

The teacher learned very quickly in the semester that his students liked zombies, and the teacher also liked zombies. He used this common ground as the launchpad to his lesson. He did not begin the lesson speaking about speeches or public speaking, avoiding that until the very end of his lesson. Instead, he went to the chalkboard and wrote the word "zombies" large enough for everyone in class to read. After he wrote the word on the board, he announced to his class that they were beginning class by talking about zombies, and the lesson began.

Lesson Overview

After writing the word on the board and telling the class they are going to talk about zombies, the teacher talked a little bit about his love of zombies: zombie movies, comics, video games, and television shows. He then asked the students what they knew about zombies. This began a dialogue. After they offered some information, the teacher gave a history of zombies. He talked about voodoo zombies and what they are. He specifically covered how they were used as a tool against an individual or small groups of people, explaining that, in this form, they were not scary unless the person was one of the people the zombie was brought back to kill.

The teacher then talked about George A. Romero, the creator of the current concept of a zombie. When he was creating the original *Night of the Living Dead* in 1968, Romero wanted zombies to be scarier. He looked at the concept of tribal warfare and the practice of cannibalism. The teacher explained that non–Jeffery Dahmer–style cannibals do not eat their victims for nourishment. Rather, it is a form of psychological warfare. The teacher then introduced the students to the idea of fighting a war in which you know your enemy is going to eat you. This is the idea that Romero added to zombies. Just by adding cannibalism to zombies, he made them into a "universal fear," something everyone is scared of.

At this point, the teacher began to talk about public speaking. He communicated that they all talk to people every day. They talk one-on-one, in small groups, over the phone, and through digital communication. The teacher then talked about adding public speaking to communication. He then compared adding cannibalism to zombies with adding public to speaking, which also creates universal fear. At this point, the students were usually ready to start examining why they were fearful or apprehensive about public speaking. The teacher usually had them write about it, share their writing with a partner or a group, and then share as a class.

References

Alvarez, L. (2011, July 5). Casey Anthony not guilty in slaying of daughter. *The New York Times*. http://www.nytimes.com/2011/07/06/us/06casey.html?pagewanted=all&_r=0

Anderson, M. L., & Taylor, H. F. (2012). *Sociology: The essentials*. Thomson Higher Education.

Ashton, K. (2015). *How to fly a horse: The secret history of creation, invention, and discovery*. Doubleday.

Blumer, H. (1969). *Symbolic interactionism: Perspectives and method*. University of California Press.

Brown, B. (2010, June). *Brene Brown: The power of vulnerability*. TED Ideas Worth Spreading. https://www.ted.com/talks/brene_brown_the_power_of_vulnerability?language=en

Brown, B. (2015). *Daring greatly: How the courage to be vulnerable transforms the way we live, love, parent, and lead*. Avery.

Carter, D. F., & Hurtado, S. (1997, October). Effects of college transition and perceptions of the campus racial climate on latino college students' sense of belonging. *Sociology of Education, 70*(4), 325–345.

Carter, P. L., & Welner, K. G. (Eds.). (2013). *Closing the opportunity gap*. Oxford University Press.

CBS News. (2008, December 15). $50B scam victims speak. *YouTube*. https://www.youtube.com/watch?v=lzAUUyd-woE

Channel 10. (2011, May 12). Planking craze. *YouTube*. https://www.youtube.com/watch?v=tRHnTFesv7c

Dix, N., Lail, A., Birnbaum, M., & Paris, J. (2020, November 1). Exploring the "at-risk" student label through the perspectives of higher education professionals. *The Qualitative Report, 25*(11), 3830–3846.

Duckworth, A. (2018). *Grit: The power of passion and perseverance*. Scribner.

Dweck, C. (2014, November). *The power of believing you can improve*. TED Ideas Worth Sharing. https://www.ted.com/talks/carol_dweck_the_power_of_believing_that_you_can_improve?language=en

Dweck, C. (2017). *Mindset: Changing the way you think to fulfil your potential*. Little Brown Book Group.

Freire, P. (1970). *Pedagogy of the oppressed*. Continuum.

Gladwell, M. (2008). *Outliers: The story of success*. Back Bay Books/Little, Brown and Company.

Hernandez, P. (2010). MSU student backgrounds: Poverty, discrimination, and dropping out of school. *Michigan Sociological Review, 24*, 97–129.

Hernandez, P. (2011). College 101: Introducing at-risk students to higher education. *NEA Higher Education Journal*, Fall, 77–89.

Hernandez, P., & Loebick, K. (2016, January 15). A future star: Challenging stereotypes of diversity. *National Education Association*. https://www.nea.org/advocating-for-change/new-from-nea/future-star-challenging-stereotypes-diversity

Hussar, B., NCES; Zhang, J., Hein, S., Wang, K., Roberts, A., Cui, J., Smith, M., AIR; Bullock Mann, F., Barmer, A., and Dilig, R., RTI (2020). The condition of education 2020 (NCES 2020-144). Washington, DC: National Center for Education Statistics. Retrieved from https://nces.ed.gov/programs/coe/indicator_cge.asp

Kirp, D. L. (2019). *The college dropout scandal*. Oxford University Press.

Macedo, D. (2000). *Introduction to Pedagogy of the oppressed* (P. Freire). Continuum.

Malcom-Piqueux, L.(2017) Taking Equity-Minded Action to Close Equity Gaps.https://www.aacu.org/peerreview/2017/Spring/Malcom-Piqueux

Mastropieri, M. A., & Scruggs, T. E. (2001). Promoting inclusion in secondary classrooms. *Learning Disability Quarterly, 24*(4), 265–274.

Mastropieri, M. A., & Scruggs, T. E. (2018). *The inclusive classroom: Strategies for effective differentiation instruction.* Pearson.

McNair, T. B., Bensimon, E. M., & Malcom-Piqueux, L. (2020). *From equity talk to equity walk: Expanding practitioner knowledge for racial justice in higher education.* Jossey-Bass.

Mediratta, K., Rausch, M. K., & Skiba, R. J. (Eds.). (2016). *Inequality in school discipline: Research and practice to reduce disparities.* Palgrave Macmillan.

Meisels, S. J., Harrington, H., McMahon, P., Dictelmiller, M., & Jablon, J. (2002). *Thinking like a teacher: Using observational assessment to improve teaching and learning.* Allyn and Bacon.

Meyer, J. (1968). *How teachers can reach the disadvantaged: Relating to the students, teaching the students, and attitudes towards the students.* Pennsylvania State University, Institute of Human Resources.

Mojica, L. (2006). Reiterations in ESL learners' academic papers: Do they contribute to lexical cohesiveness? *Asia-Pacific Education Research, 15*(1), 105–125.

National Center for Education Statistics (NCES). (2019, November 7). *Table 1. Public high school 4-year adjusted cohort graduation rate (ACGR), by race/ethnicity and selected demographic characteristics for the United States, the 50 states, the District of Columbia, and Puerto Rico: School year 2017–18.* https://nces.ed.gov/ccd/tables/ACGR_RE_and_characteristics_2017-18.asp

Northcutt, E., Higgins, J., & Combs, S. (2002). *Steck-Vaughn GED language arts, reading.* Steck-Vaughn.

Osher, D., & Kendziora, K. (2010). Building conditions for learning and healthy adolescent development: Strategic approaches. In B. Doll, W. Pfohl, & J. S. Yoon (Eds.), *Handbook of youth prevention science* (pp. 121–140). Routledge.

Riess, H. (2018). *The empathy effect: Seven neuroscience-based keys for transforming the way we live, love, work, and connect across differences.* Sounds True.

Robinson, C. (2017). Leveraging a guest speaker event to advance transformative change for at-risk student success. *Journal of Appreciative Education, 4*, 16–25.

Robinson, K. (2006, February). *Do schools kill creativity?* TED Ideas Worth Sharing. https://www.ted.com/talks/sir_ken_robinson_do_schools_kill_creativity

Robinson, K., & Aronica, L. (2015). *Creative schools: The grassroots revolution that's transforming education.* Penguin.

Robinson, S. K. (2017). *Out of our minds: The power of being creative.* John Wiley and Sons Ltd.

Rockler, N. R. (2002). Race, whiteness, "lightness," and relevance: African American and European American interpretations of jump start and the boondocks. *Critical Studies in Media Communication, 19*, 398–418.

Sachar, C. O., Cheese, M., & Richardson, S. (2019, December 31). Addressing misperceptions of underprepared students. *Global Education Review, 6*(4), 1–18.

Samuels, C. A. (2020, January 9). "At-promise"? Can a new term for "at-risk" change a student's trajectory? *Education Week.* https://www.edweek.org/policy-politics/at-promise-can-a-new-term-for-at-risk-change-a-students-trajectory/2020/01

Scene 20. (1995). *Braveheart* [DVD]. Directed by Mel Gibson. Paramount Studios.

Social Education. (1996). 1965 Alabama literacy test. *Social Education, 60*(6), 340.

Stormont, M., & Newman, C. T. (2014). *Simple strategies for teaching children at risk.* Corwin.

Strayhorn, T. L. (2019). *College students' sense of belonging: A key to educational success for all students.* Routledge.

Suzuki, S., & Dixon, T. (2006). *Zen mind, beginner's mind.* Shambhala.

Swadener, B. B. (2000). "At risk" or "at-promise?" From deficit constructions of the "other childhood" to possibilities for authentic alliances with children and families. In L. D. Soto (Ed.), *The politics of early childhood education.* Peter Lang.

Symmetry Artist. (2017). Mathematics and art come together. *Math Is Fun.* http://www.mathsisfun.com/geometry/symmetry-artist.html

Truesdale, W. (2009). *Peer coaching on the transferability of staff development: Peer coaching on the transferability of staff development to classroom practice.* VCM Verlag.

U.S. Bureau of Labor Statistics. (2019, October 21). *Median weekly earnings $606 for high school* *dropouts, $1,559 for advanced degree holders* https://www.bls.gov/opub/ted/2019/median-weekly-earnings-606-for-high-school-dropouts-1559-for-advanced-degree-holders.htm

Winterowd, R. (1985). Kenneth Burke: An annotated glossary of his terministic screen and a "statistical" survey of his major concepts. *Rhetoric Society Quarterly, 15*(3/4), 145–177.

References from the first edition

Anderson, Elijah. *Code of the Street: Decency, Violence, and the Moral Life of the Inner City.* New York: W.W. Norton, 1999.

Billings-Ladson, Gloria. "Towards a Theory of Culturally Relevant Pedagogy." *American Educational Research Journal 32*, no. 3 (1995): 465–491.

Cammarota, Julio. "Disappearing in the Houdini Education: The Experience of Race and Invisibility." *Multicultural Education 14* (2006): 2–10.

Cassidy, Wanda, and Anita Bates. "Drop-Outs and Push Outs: Finding Hope at a School That Actualizes the Ethic of Care." *American Journal of Education 112* (2005): 66–102.

Chang, Heewon. *Autoethnography as Method.* Walnut Creek, CA: Left Coast Press, 2009.

Downey, Douglas B., and Shana Pribesh. "When Race Matters: Teachers' Evaluations of Students' Classroom Behavior." *Sociology of Education 77* (2004): 267–282.

Lareau, Annete. *Unequal Childhoods: Class, Race, and Family Life.* Berkeley: University of California Press, 2003.

Marcus, R. F., & Sanders-Reio, J. (2001). The influence of attachment on school completion. *School Psychology Quarterly, 16,* 427–444.

Index

Achievement gap, 57–58
Active learning lessons, 19
Active listening skill, 9–10
Adaptability, 91–93
Administrators role, PRT, 150
Adversity, 22
Adversity talk, 156–158, 170–173
Alternative lessons, 135
    benefits, 21
    Bridge Project Packet, 181–192
    chemical bonding, 157–158
    congruent triangles, 192–198
    COVID-19 pandemic, 157–158
    creativity and, 47–50
    critical thinking and clinical judgment skills, 154–155
    defined, 8–9, 19–21, 132
    diversity, 144
    example, 19–20
    graphing linear systems, 199–205
    for history, 136–138
    for language class, Spanish, 142–145
    for mathematics, 138–142, 192–205
    "The Me You Don't Know," 98–99
    processing steps, 133–135
    professional development, 132–144
    public speaking anxiety, 206–207
    terministic screens and, 96–99
    writing assignment and, 98–99
Appropriate pace, teaching component
    assessments, 85
    conversations, 84
    defined, 14
    implementation, 83–85
    writing assignment, 84
Ashton, K., 29
Aspen Rising Presidents Fellowship, 150
Assumptions talk, 159–161
Authenticity talk, 176–177

Blumer, H., 16
Braveheart (Gibson), 80
Bridge Project Packet lesson, 181–192
Brown, B., 29, 31, 116
Burke, K., 18

Chemical bonding lesson, 157–158
Clarity, teaching component
    defined, 13
    implementation, 77–79
Classroom norms talk, 178–179
Congruent triangles lesson, 192–198
Course materials, student comfort, 47–49, 48 (figure)
COVID-19 pandemic lesson, 157–158
Creativity, 44–50
Critical thinking and clinical judgment skills lesson, 154–155

Demographic shift, 58–59
Dialogue process
    implementation of, 73–74
    liberation education model, 12
    problem-posing approach, 12–13
    Real Talk approach, 12–13
Dixon, T., 116
Duckworth, A., 29, 50
Dweck, C., 19, 29, 119

Educational models, 11–16
Effort, 93–95
Empathy, 36–40
Empowerment talk, 167–169
Enthusiasm, teaching component
    defined, 14
    implementation, 82–83
Environment, classroom, 13–15
Equity-minded perspective, 59
Exam scores, traditional *vs.* alternative lesson pedagogy, 48–49, 49 (figure)

Fake teacher, 103–104
Flexibility
   defined, 21
   implementation, 89–91
   internal structure and, 90
   racism and class discrimination, 90
   S.C.R.E.A.M. and, 21
Franklin, B., 55–56
Freire, P., 9, 11–13

General equivalency diploma (GED) exam, 6, 10
   appropriate pace and, 85
   clarity and, 79
   curriculum for, 76
   dialogue implementation, 73
   enthusiasm and, 82–83
Gibson, M., 81
Graphing linear systems lesson, 199–205
Grit, 50–55
Growth mindset, 40–44, 119–120

High school dropouts
   rates, 6
   reasons for, 5
High school equivalency program (HEP), structure of, 76
History lesson, 136–138

Imagination, 44
Immovable teachers, 56
Implementation of PRT
   adaptability, 91–93
   appropriate pace, 83–85
   clarity, 77–79
   in classrooms, 109–111
   dialogue, 73–74
   effort, 93–95
   enthusiasm, 82–83
   flexibility, 89–91
   maximized engagement, 85–87
   redundancy, 79–82
   relating to students, 74–76
   structure, 76–77
Innovation, 44
Instructor-led discussions. *See* Real Talk discussions

Language lesson, 142–145
Liberation education model, 12

Madoff, B., 199–200, 202, 204
Making inferences, 8, 80
Mastropieri, M. A., 9, 11, 13–16

Mathematics lessons
   building bridges, 138–142
   congruent triangles, 192–198
   graphing linear systems, 199–205
Maximized engagement, teaching component
   defined, 15
   Monday discussions, 86
   student presentations, 86
McNair, T. B., 59, 115
Meyer, J., 9, 11, 15–16
"The Me You Don't Know" writing assignment, 98–99
Mojica, L., 79
Movable teachers, 56
Movie clips, 207

National Center for Education Statistics (NCES), 6
New teaching strategies, 145–151
Night of the Living Dead (Romero), 207

Opportunity gap, 57–60
   Pedagogy of Real Talk, 60–66

Partnerships talk, 153–155
Pedagogy defined, 11
Pedagogy of Real Talk (PRT)
   active listening skill, 9–10
   administrators role, 150
   alternative lessons, 9–10, 19–21
   approaches, 26–28
   education models, 11–16
   educators role, 146–150
   effort, 93–95
   general equivalency diploma (GED) exam, 6, 10
   high school dropout rates, 4–5
   negative school experiences, 2–3
   opportunity gap and, 60–66
   overview, 3
   Real Talk, concept of, 8–9
   refinement of, 16–25
   research background, 7–8
   sense of belonging and, 66–70, 117
   students at-promise, 3–7, 9
   See also Real Talk approach
Pedagogy of the Oppressed (Freire), 12
Personal talk, 174–175
Pin-drop phenomenon, 107
Ponzi scheme, 199–200
Presentations, student, 86
Problem-posing approach, 12
Processing step, Real Talk, 123–128

Professional development
   alternative lessons, 132–144
   Real Talks, 115–131
PRT Institute, 114–115
   creation, 115
   training, teachers, 115–121
Public speaking lesson, 206–207

Question-based learning format, 47

Racial diversity, 57–59
Real Talk approach
   adversity, 22
   alternative lessons, 19–21
   benefits of, 26–28, 146–151
   creativity and, 29–35
   dialogue process, 12–13
   empathy and, 36–40
   flexibility, 21, 89–91
   grit, 50–55
   pedagogy defined, 11
   Real Talk discussions, 21–24
   S.C.R.E.A.M., 13–15
   strategic placement of, 24–25
   symbolic interactionism, 16–18
   terministic screens, 18–19
   themes and, 22–23
   theoretical foundations of, 11–16
   vulnerability, 29–35, 116
Real Talk discussions
   academic example, 120–121
   alternative lessons and, 108, 119
   creation of, 101–102, 123–124
   curriculum and, 101
   defined, 21–24, 99–100
   delivering, 124–125
   effects of, 103–108
   explanations, 116–117
   fake teacher, 103–104
   feedback process, 120
   growth mindset, 119–120
   pin-drop phenomenon, 107
   processing steps, 123–128
   roles of, 103
   structure of, 100–103
   teachers and students connections, 121–122
   training, teachers, 115–121
   universal themes, 22–23, 122, 125
Real Talk example
   adversity talk, 156–158, 170–173
   assumptions talk, 159–161
   classroom norms talk, 178–179

   empowerment talk, 167–169
   partnerships talk, 153–155
   personal talk, 174–175
   professional development, 128–131
   symbolism, 164–166
   themes, 180
   versatility, 162–163
Redundancy, teaching component
   alternative lesson and, 80–81
   defined, 14
   implementation, 79–82
   learning style of student, 79
   making inferences, 80
Reiss, H., 29, 36
Relating curriculum to students, 74–76
Research background, 7–8
Robinson, K., 29, 44, 118
Rockler, N. R., 18
Romero, G. A., 207

S.C.R.E.A.M.
   appropriate pace, 14, 83–85
   clarity, 13, 77–79
   dialogue, 73–74
   engagement, 15
   enthusiasm, 14, 82–83
   flexibility, 21
   maximized engagement, 85–87
   Pedagogy of Real Talk and, 13
   redundancy, 14, 79–82
   relating to students, 74–76
   structure, 13, 76–77
   variables, teaching, 13–15
Scruggs, T. E., 9, 11, 13–15
Sense of belonging, 66–70, 117
Social construction, 16–17
Social Education, 136
Sociological theory
   alternative lessons, 19–21
   flexibility, 21
   Pedagogy of Real Talk and, 16–25
   Real Talk discussions, 21–24
   symbolic interactionism, 16–18
   terministic screens, 18–19
Spectrum approach, 57
Steck-Vaughn GED textbook, 76, 80, 82, 98
Stormont, M., 4
Structure of classroom
   defined, 13
   HEP program, 76
   implementation, 76–77
   teachers and, 77

Students at-promise, 3–7
   characteristics of, 4–5
   educators role, 146–150
   enthusiasm, 14
   learning environments, 12
   Real Talk approach, 9
   risk factors, 3
   S.C.R.E.A.M. and, 13–15
   teacher's reality, 17
   teacher's success with, 15–16
Students' satisfaction and alternative lessons, 47, 47 (figure)
Successful teachers, characteristics of, 15–16
Suzuki, S., 116
Symbolic interactionism (SI), 16–18
Symbolism lesson, 164–166

Teacher's reality, 17
Teacher's success with students at-promise, 15–16
Teaching and creativity, 44–45

TED Talk, 116, 118, 119
Terministic screens
   alternative lessons, 96–99
   defined, 18–19
Themes, Real Talk example, 180
Theoretical foundations of Real Talk
   characteristics of successful teachers, 15–16
   dialogue, 12–13
   S.C.R.E.A.M., 13–15
Transforming teaching, 116
Trust, structuring Real Talks, 102

Universal themes, 22–23, 122, 125

Variables, teaching, 13–15
Versatility, 162–163
Vulnerability, 29–35
   training and, 116

Writing assignment, 98–99

Helping educators make the greatest impact

CORWIN HAS ONE MISSION: to enhance education through intentional professional learning.

We build long-term relationships with our authors, educators, clients, and associations who partner with us to develop and continuously improve the best evidence-based practices that establish and support lifelong learning.

Solutions YOU WANT | Experts YOU TRUST | Results YOU NEED

EVENTS

>>> **INSTITUTES**

Corwin Institutes provide large regional events where educators collaborate with peers and learn from industry experts. Prepare to be recharged and motivated!

corwin.com/institutes

ON-SITE PD

>>> **ON-SITE PROFESSIONAL LEARNING**

Corwin on-site PD is delivered through high-energy keynotes, practical workshops, and custom coaching services designed to support knowledge development and implementation.

corwin.com/pd

>>> **PROFESSIONAL DEVELOPMENT RESOURCE CENTER**

The PD Resource Center provides school and district PD facilitators with the tools and resources needed to deliver effective PD.

corwin.com/pdrc

ONLINE

>>> **ADVANCE**

Designed for K–12 teachers, Advance offers a range of online learning options that can qualify for graduate-level credit and apply toward license renewal.

corwin.com/advance

Contact a PD Advisor at (800) 831-6640 or visit www.corwin.com for more information